THE PSYCHOLOGY OF LEARNING:
A STUDENT WORKBOOK

THE PSYCHOLOGY OF LEARNING: A STUDENT WORKBOOK

Armando Machado
University of Minho

Francisco J. Silva
University of Redlands

Foreword by William Timberlake (Indiana University)

The psychology of learning : a student workbook / Armando Machado, Francisco J. Silva;
foreward by William Timberlake.
    p. cm.
Includes bibliographical references and index.
ISBN 0-13-091768-0
 1.Learning, Psychology of. 2. Learning, Psychology of –Problems, exercises, etc. I.
Silva, Francisco J. II Title.

BF318.M29 2003
153.1'5—dc21

2003043307

Editor-in-Chief: *Leah Jewell*
Senior Acquisitions Editor: *Jayme Heffler*
Editorial Assistants: *Kevin Doughten and Jennifer Conklin*
Executive Marketing Manager: *Sheryl Adams*
Marketing Assistant: *Jeanette Laforet*
Managing Editor: *Joanne Riker*
Production Editor: *Kathy Sleys*
Production Assistant: *Marlene Gassler*
Prepress and Manufacturing Buyer: *Tricia Kenny*
Cover Design: Kiwi Design
Cover Photo: *Dorling Kindersley Media Library*
Printer/Binder: *This book was printed and bound by Bradford & Bigelow, Inc. The cover was
printed by Phoenix Color Corp.*

Pearson Education LTD.
Pearson Education Australia PTY, Limited
Pearson Education Singapore, Pte. Ltd
Pearson Education North Asia Ltd
Pearson Education, Canada, Ltd
Pearson Educación de Mexico, S.A. de C.V.
Pearson Education–Japan
Pearson Education Malaysia, Pte. Ltd

10 9 8 7 6 5 4 3 2 1

PEARSON
Prentice
Hall

ISBN 0-13-09178-0

To Orlando, my friend.

AM

To Joe Pear, Bob Tait, and Steve Holborn for showing me the light, and Bill Timberlake for making it brighter.

FJS

CONTENTS

FOREWORD

It has been said there are two major difficulties in teaching the psychology of learning: the teacher, and the student. To this I would add a third, a general misapprehension that science is best taught as a collection of truths. Teachers reasonably want to teach relevant material using current categories; students generally want to receive and easily absorb current truths, and then recognize those truths on tests. There is nothing wrong with these desires as part of the process of science, but the content of the science of today is not necessarily the content of the science of tomorrow, just as the content of the science of yesterday is not necessarily the content today. What we know is that the path from yesterday to tomorrow goes through a common framework of formulating a possible cause, designing procedures and measures to test this formulation, representing, clarifying, checking, and interpreting the results, then reformulating the cause, and testing again.

The methods of science are very general; they don't care whether you have a well-developed theory of the basic processes of learning, or just an intuition about how people learn and remember; the sequence of activities is similar. It is these activities that raise the endeavor of science above the level of common sense. The skeptic might argue that even these activities fail to raise conclusions above the post hoc specter of "I told you so," or "I knew it all along." But this specter is not science; it is possibility masquerading as certainty, after-the-fact knowledge pretending to be understanding. Drawing it into the processes of science, requiring it to make further predictions, and then aptly testing them soon unmasks the pretension.

This workbook by Machado and Silva provides students with the language and tools of science in general and the process of studying learning in particular. It can be used with any learning text that includes areas of animal research, because its point is to teach students a process of definition, clarification, and experimentation. By the end of the book students will recognize the difference between prediction and kibitzing, between deduction and guessing, and between functional relations and deceptively simple yes/no outcomes.

The book spends a lot of initial time helping students appreciate the power and uses of graphing relationships between variables. I learned analysis of variance by doing examples by hand according to a cookbook formula. By the time I had done 10 of them, I intuitively understood how the test worked, and could apply it to different designs. Similarly, by the time a student has plotted and manipulated learning data several times, the complexity of relations between manipulations and outcomes and the importance of representation as a tool will become clear.

This workbook uses forms of active learning, convergent teaching techniques, and rapid feedback about how well the student can work with a representation or concept. The exercises are designed to move systematically to different levels of difficulty with both encouragement and mastery. The authors are sensitive to Bloom's taxonomy of instructional objectives: knowledge of facts, comprehension, application, analysis, synthesis, and evaluation. I agree with critics that Bloom's notion of a linear hierarchy of skills could profit from further analysis of the phenomena in each category along with the presumed relations among them. However, consideration of the taxonomy has the undeniable benefit of specifically focusing both the teacher and the students on different levels of interaction with the concepts and complexities of learning.

A reasonable portion of this book is devoted to helping students clarify and understand the material in a learning course. This is accomplished partly by presenting excellent summaries of concepts, measures, and models; but the primary method is leading the student through using this material in solving problems. Although not every student will routinely solve problems within science, I believe they will understand science better for thinking about the concepts and going over portions of the process, not just memorizing outcomes. Recapitulating a process of discovery (or trying and failing to recapitulate a process) is a greatly underappreciated path to original thought.

Both teacher and students should be prepared for individual differences in how easily students initially progress. Some students will get the exercises rapidly; others will struggle. Asking a group of students to plot, understand, and predict data is similar to asking them to imagine walking around the outside of their parent's home and counting the windows; the first time there will be large individual differences in their abilities. (Some people have never thought of doing such a thing, while others do it naturally.) In both cases practice and experience will reduce differences.

Dealing with the concepts and processes of learning, and generally with how to think about, analyze, and extend data, is one of the most important set of skills that can be acquired. Years after I took my first serious physics laboratory, I still remember how to think about, set up, and solve problems. Students will not forget what they learn in this book. The book itself is well constructed; the exercises are well conceived and tested. Comprehending concepts and solving problems can be work, but it is important work. If it were trivial, there would be no need for teachers, students, or books.

William Timberlake
Bloomington, IN
11/19/2002

PREFACE

Historically, the study of learning has been at the center of American and British psychology. Thousands of books and research articles have been written on the subject. Even to the casual reader, it is clear that there is no shortage of published materials on learning.

With regard to textbooks, however, we believe the currently available choices fall short in two major ways. First, the goal of condensing the large domain of learning into a textbook of manageable size often results in a dense, encyclopedic, and overwhelmingly passive presentation of historical and contemporary findings. Inevitably, perhaps, the most common remark we have heard from students of learning concerning their textbook is, "Boring!" Second, functional relations, when presented at all, are buried under a pile of facts and experimental procedures. As a consequence, students' learning is impoverished because the variation of functions is overshadowed by the variety of facts; the primary is overshadowed by the secondary. Worst of all, the skills required to understand and use functional relations -- skills crucial in learning as in any other experimental science -- are simply not taught.

One of the goals of the present workbook is to reduce or eliminate these two shortcomings. Although we do not deny the necessity of surveying the vast field of learning, or of learning basic definitions, procedures, and experimental outcomes, we believe that a course's content must also illuminate and animate the core ideas of the corresponding discipline. To that end, our workbook promotes an active, hands-on, constructivist approach to the study of learning by generally following Bloom's (1956) taxonomy of instructional objectives. Without a more active means of learning the content of learning, students are likely to resort to rote memorization alone, which results in little lasting knowledge of the fundamental ideas of learning or of the many ways to use them. In this case, the benefit of having taken a learning course is ephemeral at best, null at worst, for as Keller and Schoenfeld (1995/1950) wrote in their landmark textbook, a person who takes away from a "course nothing more than a large body of disconnected and sketchily examined items of fact, method, or theory has only a superficial and temporary advantage over the person who never attended the course" (p. LXIII).

To supplement the passive and encyclopedic content of many learning textbooks, our workbook relies heavily on the use of functional relations and their visual representation. Our work with students at a large public university (Indiana University), a small private liberal arts college (University of Redlands), and a foreign university (University of Minho) suggests that guessing, drawing, interpreting, and revising functional relations are excellent exercises to learn about learning and many aspects of the scientific approach, such as how variables are manipulated, controlled, and interrelated; how transient and steady-state analyses, or rates of change and asymptotes, point to different processes; and how theories progress from qualitative to quantitative stages. Moreover, as a take-home message, the visual representation of functional relations may be worth a thousand verbal definitions. It is one thing for students to memorize the definition of *feedback function* in the study of reinforcement schedules, but it is quite another thing for students to draw a picture that matches the definition, to identify the important properties of the picture, and then to change the picture to deal with a new problem.

To the Instructor

No book can be all things to all people. This workbook is no different. As William James (1890) remarked, "the art of being wise is the art of knowing what to overlook" (p. 369). We have chosen to overlook specialized topics and theories that are of limited utility in understanding the *fundamental* phenomena of learning. We have also chosen to overlook controversial or poorly specified interpretations, concepts, and theories whose illumination are better suited to face-to-face interchanges between students and instructors than by completing exercises in a workbook. In contrast, what we have done is select those topics that we would want all of our students -- not just those who will take more advanced courses in learning -- to remember long after a course is over. To increase the likelihood of this happening, we have replaced the passivity of memorizing definitions and procedures with the activities of graphing and interpreting functional relations -- the pillars of theory. We hope that we have chosen wisely.

Each chapter in the workbook corresponds roughly to a chapter or major sections of a chapter found in most primary learning textbooks, and begins with a brief review of the subject matter of the chapter. *The introductory notes do not replace the content of students' primary learning textbooks or lecture notes, nor do they necessarily provide a summary of these textbooks or all the information needed to complete the exercises that follow.* For that, students must use their textbooks and, perhaps more importantly, consult with their invaluable instructor and/or teaching assistant. When more extensive background information than is typically presented in textbooks is needed to solve an exercise, that information is usually presented in the exercise itself rather than in the introductions. The *primary* purpose of the introductions is to remind students of some of the topics that they read in their textbook or discussed in class. The *secondary* purpose is to, where appropriate, use the introductions to tutor students further about information that is presented in their textbooks. For example, information about cumulative records is routinely presented in learning textbooks, but detailed information teaching students on how to read these important indicators is typically absent. Similarly, most learning textbooks summarize the Rescorla-Wagner equation and the matching law, but few teach students how to use and understand these important equations. Finally, the *tertiary* purpose of the introductions is to stimulate and motivate students to reread their textbooks and/or speak with their instructors. Then, following Bloom's (1956) taxonomy of instructional objectives, exercises are generally organized in the following manner:

1. *(Basic) Knowledge* is the simplest, most basic form of learning, and amounts to recalling definitions, procedures, and facts that were learned by rote memorization.
2. *Comprehension* requires that students demonstrate an understanding of the material by translating it, interpreting it, or extrapolating it. An example might consist of interpreting the meaning of a graph or inferring the principle underlying a series of experimental outcomes.
3. *Application* occurs when students use principles or abstractions to solve novel problems. For example, using knowledge of taste aversion to condition coyotes not to kill and eat sheep.
4. *Analysis* involves reducing complex concepts or ideas into more basic units to understand how the units are related. An example would be to understand how operant with classical contingencies interact in avoidance behavior.
5. *Synthesis* is the creation of a novel idea that is informed by and rooted in existing concepts, facts, and ideas. Examples include designing an experiment to investigate a problem, or writing a paper outlining a new theory.
6. *Evaluation* consists of judging an idea against a given standard. For example, students asked to evaluate the *assumptions* of two-process theory would be demonstrating their ability to evaluate.

As much as possible, we tried to develop exercises from a constructivist approach. This approach assumes that, for information to be remembered long after a course is over, students must *discover* information and *manipulate* it by checking new information against old information, revising assumptions, beliefs, and knowledge when the old information no longer seems to work. Such student-centered instruction is the basis for the active learning we try to promote with the workbook. There is no doubt that some questions are challenging. By its very nature, discovery is difficult.

Based upon previous use with our students, the exercises are ranked roughly in order of difficulty (which tends to follow Bloom's taxonomy of instructional objectives). For undergraduates, individual instructors can assign as many or as few questions from a chapter as they wish. We can say that we have assigned every question in the workbook to undergraduates. With some help -- sometimes a lot of help -- most undergraduates in our courses have been able to solve the exercises. For graduate students, our experience suggests that they will benefit from doing all questions, even those that are seemingly easy. These questions work well for review. No student has ever accused us of not challenging them, and many comment positively about being challenged and on the usefulness of the exercises for helping them learn the course material.

How could you use this workbook? We have used it in several ways with undergraduate students. For example:

1. When prepared before class, the exercises have served as vehicles for in-class discussions of topics introduced in the primary textbook and lectures.
2. We have often interrupted a class, asked students to form groups of 3 or 4, and then attempt to solve an exercise during the next three minutes or so. A few solutions are then compared and discussed.
3. We have also used the exercises as "study guides" and then included some questions on in-class exams.
4. As an alternative to traditional midterm or final exams, exercises have also been assigned as take-home exams.
5. For learning courses fortunate enough to include a laboratory or seminar section, the exercises could serve as the catalyst for discussions or small group exercises in these sections.
6. Finally, the exercises could be assigned for extra credit.

For graduate students, the more challenging exercises in the latter half of each chapter are appropriate for an introductory graduate-level course in learning or for teaching assistants wanting a deeper understanding of learning. A Solutions Manual with answers to all exercises and additional thoughts about the problems is available from the publisher.

To the Student

In this workbook, we invite you to summarize, integrate, extend, and evaluate the most important facts, principles, and theories of learning. We challenge you to generate verbal hypotheses, to then draw them in a graph, to revise them, to consider data from various perspectives, to ponder a puzzle for five, ten, fifteen, twenty minutes and more, to relate concepts included in different chapters from your course's primary textbook, to criticize theories, to compare the content of your textbook with your common sense, and to delve into the rich subject of learning by talking with your instructor. In short, we invite you to be intellectually active.

Every exercise in the workbook has been class-tested by our students over the years. Yet, every time we teach another section of learning, new students manage to provide invaluable feedback for how to further improve the exercises. In this same tradition, we welcome any comments about

Acknowledgments

We thank the following reviewers for their helpful comments: Jennifer Higa (Texas Christian University), Peter Killeen (Arizona State University), Mark Riley (Arizona State University), Merry Sleigh (George Mason University), Peter Urcuioli (Purdue University), Cedric Williams (University of Virginia), Michael Young (Southern Illinois University), and Tom Zentall (University of Kentucky). We are also grateful to the University of Redlands's students who completed the learning course during the Spring of 2001 and 2002. Their attention to detail, willingness to tackle exercises in various forms of development, and constructive feedback helped us improve the workbook. Thanks also to Cheryl Rickabugh for the photograph of Oscar, and our editor at Prentice Hall, Jayme Heffler. Finally, a warm thank you to our families, Helena, Catarina, and Ana (AM) and Kathleen, Paulina, and Samuel (FJS), for so many things over so many years.

Armando Machado
Braga, Portugal

Francisco Silva
Redlands, California

THE PSYCHOLOGY OF LEARNING:
A STUDENT WORKBOOK

1

LEARNING AND VARIABLES

Major topics covered in the exercises of this chapter:

Learning, independent variables, dependent variables, confounding variables, operational definitions

The goal of studying learning

Learning refers to a heterogeneous set of processes that evolved in animals because these processes adapted them to changes in their environments. These processes can produce relatively permanent changes in behavior, and are brought into play by interactions between the animal and its surroundings. For instance, a moving nematode (a tiny worm) that stops momentarily or reverses its motion when it experiences a vibration will cease doing so if the vibration occurs repeatedly. After finding food, foraging bees return to the hive and then perform an intricate "dance" the orientation and speed of which change with the direction and distance of the food source from the hive; based on that dance, other bees can locate the food. Hungry house cats mew in the presence of their owners, who then feed the animals. In all of these examples, the organism's behavior is showing the effects of particular interactions between itself and its environment. Classifying distinct types of interactions, identifying their elements, quantifying their static and dynamic properties, and describing how their cumulative effects are expressed is the subject matter of the psychology of learning.

Behavior is lawful

An important assumption made by scientists who study learning is that behavior is lawful. That is to say, there are causes for behavior and, all else being equal, the same causes produce the same effects on behavior. But just because behavior is caused by something, it does not follow that the behavior in question is necessarily automatic, or that its occurrence is guaranteed or inevitable. Often, when we say that event A causes behavior B, we mean simply that behavior B is more likely to occur when event A happens than when it does not. Why do learning theorists make this assumption? The answer is simple but not necessarily obvious. First, the history of science and its many achievements provide overwhelming evidence that this assumption is worth entertaining. Second, it would be pointless to study why people and animals do what they do if there were no causes for their actions. Third, the assumption of behavioral lawfulness gives us hope that the behavior of people and animals can be predicted, understood, and improved.

Independent, dependent, and confounding variables

Before scientists can classify types of environment-behavior interactions, quantify their properties, and describe how their cumulative effects are expressed, they need to identify the elements of these interactions -- *variables* -- and how these variables are related to one another -- *functional relations.*[1] A variable is anything that can take at least two values: Weight, temperature, IQ, socioeconomic status, and religious preference are examples of variables. In fact, hardly anything in nature happens without measurable variation.

Changes in one variable may be associated with changes in another variable and when this happens we say the two variables are related. For example, the probability of someone having lung cancer is related to the number of cigarettes the person smokes; the number of annual highway accidents is related to the annual amount of precipitation; the speed at which a rat runs down a straight-alley runway to get a piece of food is related to the time since the animal's last meal.[2]

In an experiment, when one variable depends on another variable, we say that the first variable is a *dependent variable.* Because the speed of running down the alley depends on how long it has been since the rat's last meal, the rat's running speed is the dependent variable. A variable that might cause changes in the dependent variable is termed the *independent variable.* In the previous example, the time since the rat's last meal is the independent variable because we believe that it will influence the rat's running speed. Psychologists actively change or manipulate independent variables to examine and measure their effects on dependent variables.

A variable that affects the dependent variable but which (a) is not the independent variable, and (b) is unknown to the experimenter or he cannot control it is termed a *confounding variable.* To illustrate, a rat runs faster down the alley for some types of food than others. Type of food is therefore a potential confounding variable because, if the experimenter does not control it, the variable will affect running speed. The experimenter will be unable to say whether *time since the last meal* or *type of food* affected the rat's running speed. In this example, the experimenter could control the confounding variable by keeping it constant: The animal would always receive the same food at the end of the alley.

As summarized in Table 1.1, experimenters act in specific ways toward each type of variable.

Table 1.1

Variable		Action
Independent	→	Manipulate
Confounding	→	Control
Dependent	→	Measure

Operational definitions

To establish a functional relation between variables, those variables must first be measured. An *operational definition* is a description of a variable in terms of the operations used to establish or measure that variable. For example, an operational definition of food deprivation is the amount of time since an animal last ate. As a second example, consider a list of foreign words a student must memorize. An operational definition of the difficulty of the list is provided by the number of times the student needs to read the list before she can evoke all the words correctly. As a third example, a psychologist might define a baby's reaction of surprise to an object by the amount of time the baby looks at the object before looking away for more than two seconds. Note that the three operational definitions specify how to establish and measure a potentially ambiguous concept, the degree of food deprivation, the difficulty of a list of words, or the baby's reaction of surprise.

---

[1] Functional relations are studied in the next chapter.
[2] Some people believe that the number of annual births in a particular city is related to the number of storks that annually cross the skies of that city. What do you think about this relation?

EXERCISES

1-1: Consider the following example. An athlete broke both of his arms while playing hockey. During the 8 weeks that his arms were in casts, he could not play sports, ride a bicycle, or shake hands. It is clear that the injury caused the athlete's behavior to change (e.g., no playing sports, no riding a bike, no shaking hands). It's also clear that these and other changes in his behavior lasted for a relatively long time (8 weeks).

1-1.1: Write out the definition of learning provided in your textbook.

1-1.2: With reference to the definition you copied from your textbook, discuss whether the change in the athlete's behavior is an instance of learning. [Hint: Even though the description in exercise **1-1** might seem consistent with the definition of learning written in your textbook -- as well as with the definition provided in the introduction to this chapter -- consider whether all changes in behavior are the result of learning.]

1-2: The presence of confounding variables can lead people to reach illogical conclusions. To illustrate, consider the following conversation between two friends:

Mark: "John, I finally figured out why I get drunk!"
John: "What's the reason?"
Mark: "Well, three nights ago I drank two glasses of scotch with water and felt drunk; two nights ago I had a bit of rum with water and felt drunk; last night I changed to gin with water and felt drunk again...."
John: "So?"
Mark: "Don't you get it?"
John: "No."
Mark: "It's the water!"

With reference to confounding variables, what is wrong with Mark's conclusion?

1-3: For each case below, (a) identify the independent variable, (b) identify the dependent variable, and (c) describe in one or two sentences how the independent and dependent variables are related. In each case, be sure to check your reasoning against the definitions of independent, dependent, and confounding variables.

Case 1: Ivan Pavlov, a Russian physiologist, observed that the amount a dog salivated to a ringing bell increased, up to a point, with an increase in the number of conditioning trials (i.e., pairings of the bell with food placed in the dog's mouth).

Case 2: A psychologist observed that the more a rat was deprived of food (operationally defined as the number of hours since the rat's last meal), the faster it ran down an alley with a piece of food at the end.

Case 3: Hermann Ebbinghaus, a famous 19th century psychologist who studied memory, observed that the degree of forgetting information increases with the amount of time since the person last learned the information. [Hint: In this example, you will need to create a plausible measure of forgetting.]

1-4: Imagine that you have been asked to study how alcohol affects driving ability.

1-4.1: How do you think alcohol consumption will affect driving ability? (This is your hypothesis.)

1-4.2: Design a *plausible* and *simple* experiment to test your hypothesis.

1-4.3: Identify the independent variable, dependent variable, and a potential confounding variable in your experiment.

1-4.4: How could you control the confounding variable you identified?

1-5: Operationally define each of the following concepts:

1-5.1: The *amount of practice* riding a bike.

1-5.2:   The *ability* to play golf.

1-5.3:   The degree of a rat's *mastery* of a maze.

1-5.4:   A child's *resistance* to *frustration*. (Note that there are two concepts to define: resistance and frustration.)

2

GRAPHS AND FUNCTIONS

Major topics covered in the exercises of this chapter:

Functional relations, graphs, linear and nonlinear relations, positive and negative relations, positively and negatively accelerated relations

Functional relations

When changes in the independent variable cause orderly changes in the dependent variable, we say that there is a *functional relation* between the two variables. That is, the quantity of the dependent variable is a function of the quantity of the independent variable. Scientists who study learning are interested in identifying and understanding functional relations. To a large extent, science consists of replacing the variety of facts by the variation of functions. Because functional relations are often presented in graphs, we will outline some steps for drawing line graphs -- the most common type used for showing functional relations and the most common type used in this workbook.

Drawing graphs

Like any other skill, drawing functional relations requires some practice to do it right. We outline below 10 steps for drawing good graphs. The hypothetical example that will guide us is as follows: We want to know how the temperature of an old oven changes with time since it was switched on. We assume that a person placed a thermometer inside the oven, and then turned on the oven by setting its thermostat to 150 degrees. Afterwards, she read the thermometer every 5 minutes and obtained the data shown in Table 2.1.

Table 2.1

Time (in minutes)	Temperature (in Celsius)
0	20
5	56
10	87
15	100
20	118
25	129
30	133
35	138
40	142
45	144
50	146

To see how the oven's temperature (dependent variable, y) varied with time since the oven was switched on (independent variable, x), we will draw a graph.

1. Draw the axes.

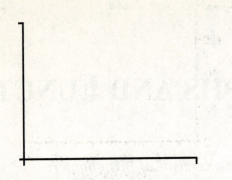

2. Determine the origin and the end values. When appropriate, have the two axes intersecting at the zero-zero point. Be careful to consider the meaning of the origin and end values. For example, if plotting a person's height (y) as a function of her age (x), it makes no sense to set the end values for height at 15 feet or age at 200 years.

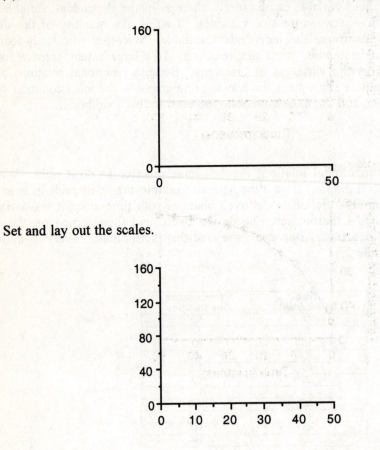

3. Set and lay out the scales.

4. Label the axes appropriately, being sure to include the units of measurement.

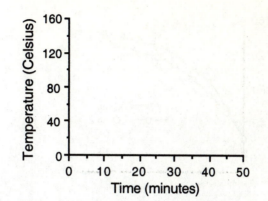

5. Plot the data points.

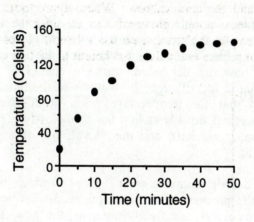

6. Connect the data points.

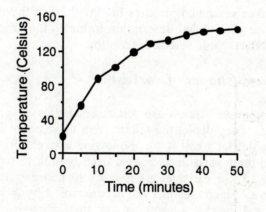

7.   Add a legend if there is more than one line or curve[1] in a graph.

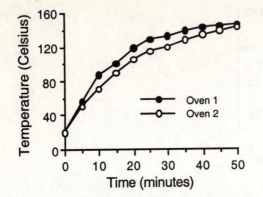

8.   Read the curves by describing in words what you see in the graph. One way to do this is to start with the independent variable, move from left to right, as it were, and then describe how the dependent variable changes. Let us illustrate the approach with the curve for Oven 1 above: "As the time since the oven was turned on increases [we go from left to right along the independent variable], the oven's temperature also increases [we describe how the dependent variable changes]." After this general description, we may want to identify specific features of the functional relation. In the example, we could say that the temperature starts at 20 degrees, presumably the ambient temperature, increases quickly at first but then slowly (i.e., as we explain later, in a negatively accelerated fashion), and then levels off at about 150 degrees, the setting of the thermostat.

9.   Ask yourself: Does my description make sense? Does it match the graph? To answer the questions, reverse the process: Hide the graph, read what you wrote aloud, draw a curve *based on what you wrote*, and finally compare the new curve with the original one.

10. If your description makes sense and matches the graph, then the graph is complete. If it does not, either revise your verbal description to match the graph or revise the graph so that it accurately reflects your verbal description.

Common functional relations (shapes of curves)

Variables can be related in many ways. Below are some schematics of general functional relations common in the area of learning. They depict the relationship between an independent variable (let's call it x) and a dependent variable (let's call it y). Following convention, we assume the x variable increases from left to right, and the y variable increases from bottom to top.

   Linear Relations. In Fig 2.1, the variables are *linearly* related because their functional relation plots as a straight line.[2] In curve A, increases in x are accompanied by increases in y -- the variables change in the same direction, and for that reason we say they are *positively* related. In curve B, increases in x are accompanied by decreases in y -- the variables move in opposite directions, and we say they are *negatively* related.

---

[1] Following convention and for simplicity, we refer to all plots that appear in line graphs as "curves" even though plots of data and functions sometimes produce linear (i.e., straight line) relations.
[2] For students who are mathematically inclined, this relation is expressed in the form $y(x) = mx + b$.

Figure 2.1

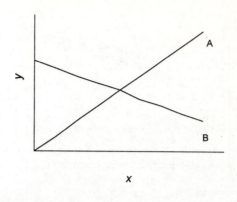

Because some students have difficulty with the concept of linear relations, curve A is redrawn in Fig 2.2 to more clearly illustrate how changes in x relate to changes in y. In the figure, two changes in x are labeled Δx; they are equal. The corresponding changes in y are labeled Δy_1 and Δy_2. Because the relation between y and x is linear, the two changes in y are also equal, that is, $\Delta y_1 = \Delta y_2$.

Figure 2.2

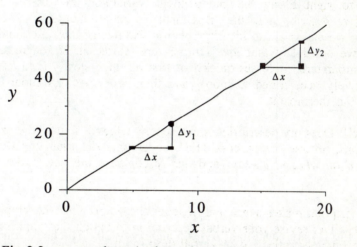

The values of Δx in Fig 2.2 are equal to 4; the values of Δy_1 and Δy_2 are 12. To check your understanding, redraw curve B (the negative, linear relation) in a format similar to the preceding graph. If you do it correctly, then you will see that equal increments in x produce equal *decrements* in y.

   Positively Accelerating Relations. In Fig 2.3 the relations are *nonlinear*; that is, they do not plot as straight lines. The variables in curve C are positively related, whereas those in curve D are negatively related. Pay attention now to the pattern of growth in C: When x is small, an increase in x is accompanied by a small increase in y, but when x is large, the same increase in x is accompanied by a larger increase in y. That is, if we increase the independent variable x by the same amount, we get larger and larger increments on the dependent variable y. The curve is speeding up, as it were. When this pattern of change holds we say the curve is *positively accelerated*.[3] In curve D the situation is similar except that y decreases with x. That is, if we consider only the magnitude of the changes in y (i.e., disregard their sign), then we get larger and larger changes in y as we increase x by the same amount.

---

[3] Why do we speak of acceleration here? Think of x as time and y as distance covered. How is speed changing in C? What do we call a change in speed?

Figure 2.3

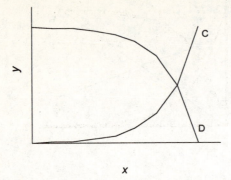

Curve C is redrawn in Fig 2.4 to more clearly illustrate how equal increments in x produce progressively larger increments in y.

Figure 2.4

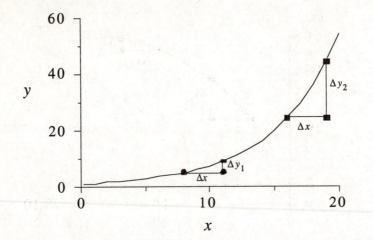

The values of Δx in Fig 2.4 are equal to 4; $\Delta y_1 = 5$ and $\Delta y_2 = 20$. To check your understanding, redraw curve D in a format similar to the preceding graph. Illustrate how equal increments in x produce progressively larger decrements (in absolute value) in y.

    Negatively Accelerating Relations. In Fig 2.5, the variables are again nonlinearly related (why?). In curve E they are positively related, whereas in curve F they are negatively related (why?). Note that for small values of x, changes in x cause large changes in y; however, for large values of x, changes in x cause small changes in y. That is, if we increase the independent variable x by the same amount, we get smaller and smaller increments (in E) or decrements (in F) for the dependent variable y. The curve is slowing down, as it were. When this pattern of change occurs we say the curve is *negatively accelerated.*

Figure 2.5

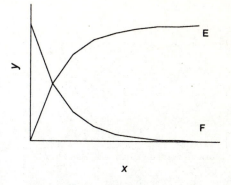

Again, because students often have difficulty with the concept of acceleration, curve E is redrawn in Fig 2.6 to more clearly illustrate how equal increments in x produce progressively smaller increments in y.

Figure 2.6

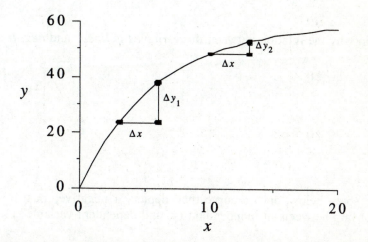

The values of Δx in Fig 2.4 are equal to 4; $\Delta y_1 = 15$ and $\Delta y_2 = 5$. To check your understanding, redraw curve F and show that equal increments in x produce progressively smaller decrements in y.

To further check your understanding, answer the following question: Explain why the variables in curve E are *positively* related, but the curve is *negatively* accelerated. Conversely, why do we say the variables in curve F are *negatively* related and the curve is *negatively* accelerated?

EXERCISES

2-1: In the introduction to this chapter, you were prompted to check your understanding of the material by redrawing some graphs and to think about some questions pertaining to functional relations. If you have not already done so, now you have the opportunity to explicitly answer those questions.

2-1.1: In the space below, draw a curve that depicts a negative linear relationship between an independent variable (x) and a dependent variable (y).

2-1.2: Explain why the relation between the variables is *linear* and *negative*.

2-1.3: In the space below, draw a curve that depicts a negative, positively accelerating relationship between an independent (*x*) and dependent variable (*y*).

2-1.4:   Explain why the relation between the variables is *negative* but the curve is *positively accelerated*.

2-1.5:   In the space below, draw a curve that depicts a negative, negatively accelerating relationship between an independent (*x*) and dependent variable (*y*). [Hint: You've seen this before.]

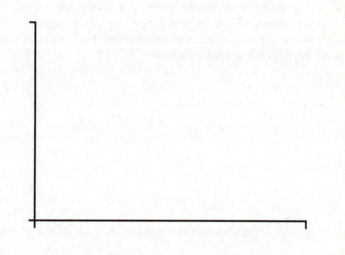

2-1.6:   Explain why the relation between the variables is *negative* and the curve is *negatively accelerated*.

2-2:   We mentioned that a positive functional relation means that the two variables change in the same direction. For example, the ability to play golf is *positively* related to amount of practice playing the game because when practice increases the ability to play the game also increases. But consider the following: To determine empirically how the ability to play golf varies with amount of practice, you start by operationally defining the two variables: *amount of practice* is defined as the number of hours a person spends practicing the game; *ability to play golf* is defined as the number of strokes required to finish 18 holes. Equipped with these definitions, you then conduct an experiment and obtain the following relation:

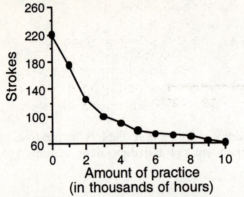

According to the graph, as the number of hours spent practicing increases, the number of strokes required to finish 18 holes decreases. That is, the graph depicts a *negative* relation, not a positive one as we initially stated. There appears to be a contradiction between our initial statement and the results. Explain why there really isn't a contradiction.

2-3: In the space next to graphs, identify what is wrong with each of the graphs below:

A

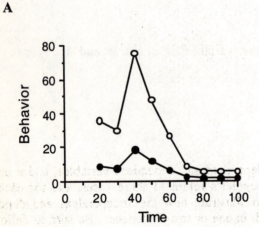

B

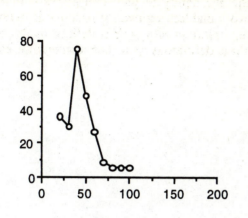

C

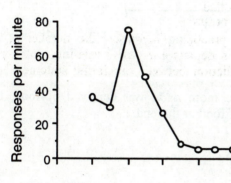

D

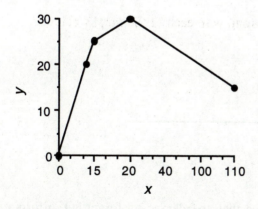

2-4: In the previous chapter, you identified the independent and dependent variables, and a possible confounding variable for each of the cases below. Now let's return to these cases, and for each one, do the following: (a) draw a function in a graph to illustrate how the independent and dependent variables are related, and then (b) describe your graph in one or two sentences. Be sure to follow the 10 steps for making graphs.

2-4.1:   Case 1: Ivan Pavlov observed that the amount a dog salivated increased, up to a point, with an increase in the number of conditioning trials.

2-4.2:   Case 2: A psychologist observed that the more a rat was deprived of food, the faster it ran down an alley with a piece of food at the end.

2-4.3:   Case 3: Hermann Ebbinghaus observed that the degree of forgetting information increases with the amount of time since the person last learned the information.

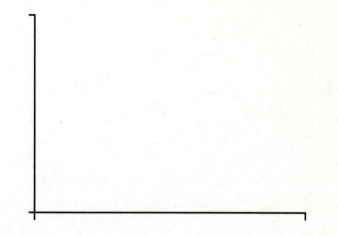

2-5: In the previous chapter, you were also asked to design a study of how alcohol affects driving ability. In the space below, illustrate your hypothesis in graphical form.

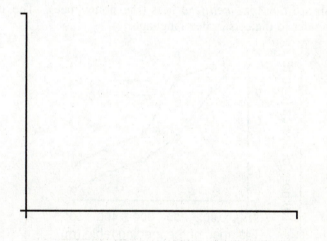

2-6: Imagine the following scenario: It is the year 1650 and you are in London, England, working for a life insurance company. Your task is to construct London's first mortality table, which provides statistical information about when people die. You begin by randomly selecting 100 newborns, and then follow their lives to record the age at which each person dies.

Once you have this information, draw a plausible curve showing how the *Number of People Still Alive* varies with *Age* (i.e., of the 100 people, some number are still alive after 0, 10, 20, ... , N years). Then, on the same graph, draw a curve for the same sort of data collected during the latter part of the 20th century. [Hint: To draw plausible curves, consider differences in infant mortality and medical care between the 17th and 20th centuries.]

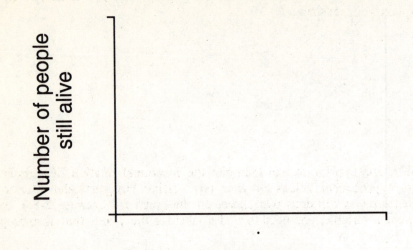

Age (years)

2-7: When a worker bee finds a good source of food, it communicates its finding to other bees in its hive by means of a "tail-wagging dance," which consists of, among other variations, walking rapidly in a circle by first turning to the right and then to the left in a horizontal figure-8 pattern. The rhythm of the dance indicates the distance from the hive to the food source. The graph below shows the "code" for two strains of the *Apis mellifera* bees (the honey bee). The difference between them has led some experts to refer to dialects in bee language.

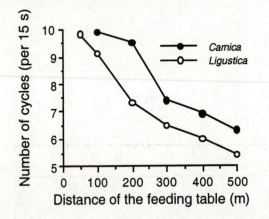

2-7.1: Consider now that an experimenter puts two bees of different strains together. One of them (let's call it a *Ligustica*) has found food at 200 m from the hive. Using the graph above, predict where the other bee (let's call it a *Carnica*) will search for food. Explain your reasoning.

2-7.2: Now consider the reverse situation: How far away from the hive will a *Ligustica* search for food if a *Carnica* danced after having found food 200 m away from the hive? Explain your reasoning.

2-8: Identify the variables and their units, and then plot the functional relation in a graph for each of the following. Create hypothetical values for your axes. [Hint: Pay particular attention to the labeling of the *y*-axis. Because you will draw two curves on the graph for exercise **2-8.3**, each curve corresponding to a different *y* variable, you need to find a label for the *y*-axis that is appropriate for both.]

2-8.1: As the number of species on an island increases, the total immigration rate (λ, defined as the number of new species arriving per year) decreases linearly.

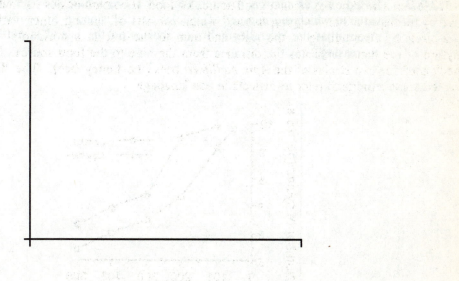

2-8.2: As the number of species on an island increases, the total extinction rate (μ, defined as the number of species on the island that become extinct each year) increases linearly.

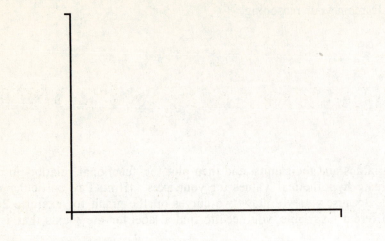

2-8.3: Based on your answers to exercises **2-8.1** and **2-8.2**, show in the graph below the value at which the number of species on the island is at equilibrium.[4] Equilibrium means that the overall number of species on the island is neither increasing nor decreasing.

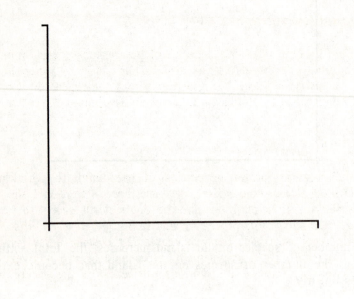

---

[4] We are assuming that the only relevant factors are immigration and extinction.

3

HABITUATION AND ITS PROPERTIES

Major topics covered in the exercises of this chapter:

Habituation, properties of habituation, stimulus generalization, stimulus specificity, spontaneous recovery

What is habituation?

Habituation is the waning of a response to a stimulus due to repeated presentations of that stimulus. The stimulus is generally neutral or harmless. Psychologists believe that *every* animal species shows habituation, a remarkable fact that attests to the importance of habituation in an animal's adaptation to its environment. You can glimpse at the importance of habituation by imagining what it would be like for a human or an animal to respond to each and every stimulus in its world.

Illustrating habituation in a graph

Habituation can be shown by plotting some measure of the response (e.g., intensity, probability) on the *y*-axis against the number of stimulus presentations on the *x*-axis. When habituation occurs, the resulting curve shows a decrease in the response as the stimulus is repeatedly presented. We will ask you to interpret and draw graphs of habituation in the exercises below.

Properties of habituation

You can understand the most important properties of habituation by thinking about the startle response of a dog to a loud, unexpected noise. Suppose that on Session 1 the noise is presented 4 times, with 10 seconds between presentations, and the dog's startle response to each presentation is measured. Fig 3.1 is a schematic of this procedure and its hypothetical results. In the left oval, the magnitude of the startle response (black bars) decreases as the same noise (white bars) is repeated. The right oval shows the results if the experiment is repeated after a recovery period of 24 hours. Examine the figure closely, and relate the various attributes of the figure to the properties of habituation listed below.

Figure 3.1

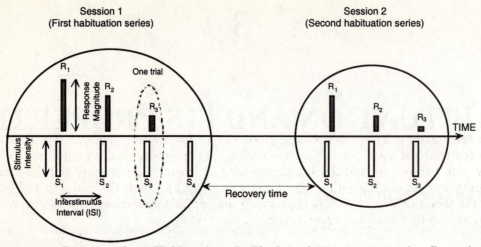

Spontaneous Recovery from Habituation. In Fig 3.1, the response to the first stimulus during the second habituation series is stronger than the response to the last stimulus during the first habituation series. This means that the passage of time *without the presentation of the stimulus* brought the strength of the habituated response closer to its original value. That is, the passage of time caused the recovery of the response. More generally, the degree of spontaneous recovery increases with the duration of the recovery interval.

Relearning Effect. In Figure 3.1, the response decreased faster during the second habituation series than during the first series. More generally, if a response habituates and is then allowed to recover, (re)habituation of the response is typically faster. Note that this property refers to the rate or speed that the response wanes.

Interstimulus Interval (ISI) Effect. Shorter ISIs lead to faster habituation and faster recovery from habituation than do longer ISIs.

Stimulus Intensity Effect. Responses to strong stimuli wane more slowly than responses to weak stimuli.

Stimulus Generalization and Stimulus Specificity of Habituation. Habituation to a stimulus generalizes to similar stimuli. Suppose a noise is presented until the startle response habituates. Then a noise differing from the original noise along some dimension is presented. If the response to the new stimulus equals, or differs only slightly from, the response to the original stimulus, then we say there was substantial generalization of habituation or, equivalently, low stimulus specificity. Conversely, if the responses differ markedly, then we say there was little generalization or high stimulus specificity

Note that stimulus generalization and stimulus specificity are the two sides of one coin: They are the same property seen from different perspectives. To emphasize the degree of similarity between the two stimuli, one talks about stimulus generalization; to emphasize the degree of dissimilarity, one talks about stimulus specificity.

EXERCISES

3-1: Johnny is planning to rent a house located near railroad tracks. During a visit to the house, the landlord assured Johnny that the train passed only once a day, albeit during the night. "But don't worry, Johnny," said the landlord, "you will get used to it within 10 days." After some thinking, Johnny replied: "Well, then, instead of moving in today I'll move in 10 days from now. How about that?" With reference to the operations necessary for producing habituation, what is wrong with Johnny's solution?

3-2: With reference to the operations and properties of habituation, interpret the following story: "One day a fox who had never seen a lion was walking in the woods. Suddenly the king of the beasts stood in the path before him, and the fox almost died of fright. He ran away and hid himself in his den. The next time he came upon the lion he merely paused to allow the majestic beast to pass by. The third time they met the fox boldly approached the lion and passed the time of day with him and asked about his family's health." From *Aesop's fables* (1999).

3-3: Explain how habituation could cause a person to stop listening to a CD that was so wonderful when it was first purchased, to tire of watching the same movie, and to become bored with having sex with the same partner. Then, with reference to the properties of habituation, describe what could be done in *each* case to prevent habituation or to dishabituate behavior.

3-4: Male three-spined stickleback are territorial fish. When one male invades the territory of another male, the invader is attacked ferociously. However, the attacking response, which consists mainly of biting, may habituate.

To study this phenomenon, a male stickleback was placed in a glass box. Let's call this fish, the Intruder. The box was then placed into the left side of another male stickleback's territory. Let's call this fish, the Territory Owner. The biting response of the Territory Owner, which was restricted to strikes at the glass box, was measured every two minutes. The results of a typical male stickleback are presented in the left panel of the graph below.

In the next session, either the same or a different Intruder was placed in the glass box, and then the box was presented either in the same (left) side of the territory or the different (right) side. A typical Territory Owner's responses to these four stimulus conditions -- [1] same Intruder presented in the same side of the territory, [2] same Intruder presented in the different side, [3] different (new) Intruder presented in the same side, and [4] different (new) Intruder presented in the different side -- are displayed in the right panel. For simplicity, assume that the Intruder's behavior does not change across sessions.

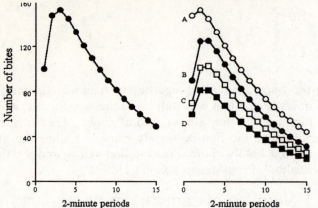

Complete the table below by matching the four curves in the right panel of the graph to the four stimulus conditions.

Curve	Stimulus
A	
B	
C	
D	

Explain your reasoning.

3-5: Imagine that you have been asked to design a 2-group experiment to test the ISI property of habituation. Draw your predictions in the graph below. [Hint: Because there are two groups, you will need two curves. Label each curve.]

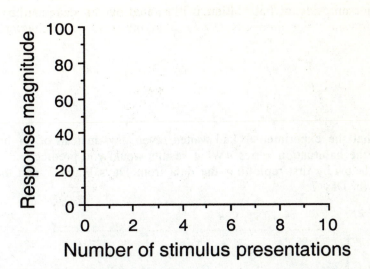

3-6: Each of the 11 groups of rats below was presented with a noise until there was little, if any, startle response to the noise. Then, following a recovery period that differed for each group, the same noise was again presented to the animals. Explain the graph below. What property of habituation does it illustrate?

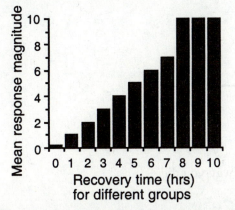

3.7: In an experiment on habituation, crabs were presented with a "predatory" shadow for 20 trials, and their escape response was recorded until it habituated (Day 1, depicted in the graphs below). After 24 hours, the experiment was repeated (Day 2, depicted in the graphs). The results for a group of crabs are shown in the graphs below. The dependent measure in the left panel is *mean escape score*; the dependent measure in the right panel is *% of maximum score*. We'll say more about the differences between these dependent measures later in exercise 3-7.4.

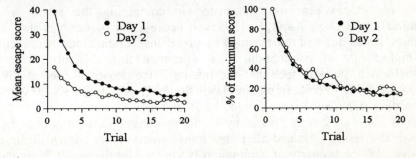

3-7.1: What major property of habituation is illustrated by the data in the left graph? Explain.

3-7.2: Suppose that the experimenter had waited seven days instead of 24 hours before repeating the habituation series. What results would you predict? Plot them in the graph below by first replotting the data from Days 1 and 2, and then drawing the curve for Day 7.

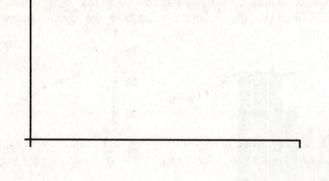

3-7.3: Explain why you drew the curve for Day 7 the way you did.

3-7.4: The researchers also were interested in comparing the rates, or speeds, of habituation in Days 1 and 2. However, because the two curves start at different values, it was difficult to determine by visual inspection alone which curve showed a higher *rate* of habituation. To eliminate this difficulty, the researchers transformed the data such that the maximum response of each day was given a score of 100%. For example, in Day 1 the maximum mean score was 39. Hence, all values from Day 1 were divided by 39 and then multiplied by 100. Similarly, all values from Day 2 were divided by 18, its maximum value, and then multiplied by 100. The results obtained after this transformation are shown in the right graph above. Which property of habituation is violated by the results? Explain.

3-8: The graphs below show the response of four groups of nematodes (tiny soil worms called *Vorticella convallaria*) to a mechanical or an electrical stimulus. In the left panel, the Experimental group experienced several presentations of a mechanical stimulus during the first 300 seconds and then presentations of an electrical stimulus thereafter; the Control group experienced only presentations of the electrical stimulus. In the right panel, another Experimental group was presented first with the electrical stimulus and then the mechanical stimulus; the other Control group in this case experienced only the mechanical stimulus.

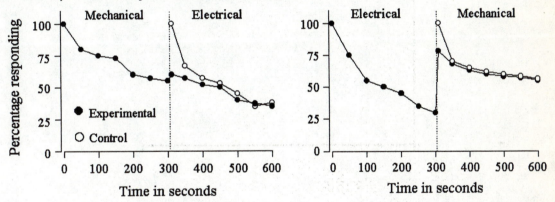

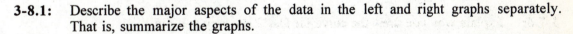

3-8.1: Describe the major aspects of the data in the left and right graphs separately. That is, summarize the graphs.

3-8.2: Identify the property or properties of habituation illustrated by the data in the right panels of each graph. Explain your reasoning.

3-8.3:   What is unusual about the results of this study? Explain. [Hint: Think about if and when stimulus specificity occurred.]

4

BASIC PRINCIPLES OF PAVLOVIAN CONDITIONING

Major topics covered in the exercises of this chapter:

Pavlovian conditioning, unconditional stimulus (US), conditional stimulus (CS), unconditional response (UR), conditional response (CR), extinction of a CR, spontaneous recovery of a CR, (conditional) stimulus generalization, stimulus discrimination, CS-US arrangements, higher-order conditioning

Pavlovian conditioning

Food and water, predators and prey, mates and offspring, and escape routes and shelter are some of the primary determiners of survival and reproduction. As such, it is reasonable to attribute great evolutionary advantage to animals capable of anticipating them. For all animals, specific sounds, sights, or odor trails, places or times of occurrence, or more complex sequences and configurations of stimuli might be reliably correlated with biologically important events. If an animal could learn the correlational texture of its world (i.e., the relationships among events), then it would have the advantage of responding one way when a stimulus predicts an important event and in another way when a stimulus does not.

The pioneering work examining how an animal learns the correlation between a neutral and a biologically important stimulus was conducted by Ivan Pavlov, the famous Russian physiologist and 1904 Nobel Prize winner, who reduced the problem to its bare essentials: A tone reliably preceded a bit of meat powder delivered to the mouth of a hungry dog. Of interest was the animal's behavior during the tone. Initially, when the tone was presented the dog pricked up its ears and looked in the direction of the source of the tone, but, importantly, it did not salivate. After a few pairings of the tone and food, the orienting response elicited by the tone ceased (habituation had set in) and a new response during the tone began to occur -- salivation. Because food-in-the-mouth elicited copious salivation without any previous training, Pavlov called food-in-the-mouth the *unconditional stimulus*, or US, and salivation because of food the *unconditional response*, or UR. As the quantity and quality of salivation to the tone depended on (i.e., was conditional upon) the prior history of pairings of the tone with food, Pavlov called the salivation to the tone a *conditional response*, or CR, and the tone a *conditional stimulus*, or CS. The study of how behavior changes when two or more stimuli are paired, as in the preceding example, is known as Pavlovian conditioning. With this and similar laboratory preparations, Pavlov and many other subsequent researchers have tried to understand how animals learn the cuing function of stimuli. Summaries of basic phenomena follow.

Pavlovian extinction

If, after the tone elicits salivation reliably, it is presented without the food, then the dog will eventually stop salivating during the tone. That is, when the CS no longer predicts the US, the CR weakens and might eventually disappear. Through acquisition and extinction processes, animals adjust to changes in the pattern of events in their environment.

Spontaneous recovery of a conditional response

If the experimenter allows the dog to rest for, say, 24 hours after extinction training, and then presents the tone again, the animal that had stopped salivating to the tone may now again salivate to it. That is, the CR spontaneously recovers. The passage of time undoes some of the effects of extinction.

(Conditional) stimulus generalization

Having learned to salivate to a specific tone, the dog also will salivate to similar tones. That is, a CR will be elicited by the original stimulus as well as similar stimuli; however, the more different these other stimuli are from the original CS, the weaker the CR they elicit.

(Conditional) stimulus discrimination

When Pavlov alternated two tones during training and paired one, but not the other, with food, his dogs eventually salivated only to the tone paired with food. That is, if one stimulus (CS+) is paired with a US, but another stimulus (CS-) is not, then the CR will occur only or mainly in the presence of the CS+.

EXERCISES

4-1: With reference to an example provided in your textbook or by your instructor, distinguish among an *unconditional stimulus (US)*, an *unconditional response (UR)*, a *conditional stimulus (CS)*, and a *conditional response (CR)*.

4-2: The following are well-known procedures or preparations used to study Pavlovian conditioning: (a) eye-blink conditioning in rabbits and humans, (b) conditioned suppression (also known as *conditioned emotional fear* or *fear conditioning*), (c) galvanic skin response (GSR) or electrodermal response conditioning, and (d) taste or flavor aversion conditioning. For each preparation, briefly describe the preparation and then identify the CS, US, CR, and UR.

4-3: What distinguishes whether an animal is showing *stimulus generalization* or *stimulus discrimination*? [Hint: In trying to answer this question, think about whether there is a point at which generalization becomes discrimination, or vice versa. If there is no such point, then how are stimulus generalization and stimulus discrimination related? Need another hint? Think about whether there is a point at which the color red becomes the color orange.]

4-4: *Forgetting* is, in part, the inability to produce the correct action in response to a particular stimulus even though the correct action has previously been learned. Examples in everyday life are common, such as when someone asks "Who is the Vice President of the United States?" and the person answers "I don't remember."

In Pavlovian *extinction*, a CS fails to elicit a CR. Are forgetting and extinction the same phenomena? If so, how are they similar? If not, how are they different? [Hint: Think about the operations or procedures that create forgetting versus extinction.]

4-5: There are several basic ways to present a CS and US. For example, the CS could occur immediately before the US (which is generally referred to as *forward* or *delay* conditioning) or it could occur just after the US (which is generally referred to as *backward* conditioning). Also, the CS could be followed by a trace or gap in time before the US is presented (*trace* conditioning) or the two stimuli could occur simultaneously (*simultaneous* conditioning). These are illustrated below in what is sometimes called a deflection diagram. Reading from left to right, the vertical bars, or deflections, denote when a CS and a US were presented and removed, respectively.

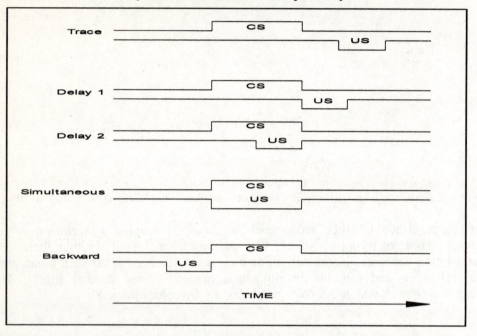

In general, delay conditioning produces the *fastest* and *strongest* conditioning, measured, say, in terms of the percentage of CSs with a CR. Trace conditioning produces slower and weaker conditioning; simultaneous and backward conditioning produce the slowest and weakest conditioning, often even producing what is referred to as *inhibitory conditioning* (more about this in the next chapter). Placing four curves on a single graph, draw the acquisition of a CR during each of these procedures (i.e., trace, delay, simultaneous, and backward conditioning).

4-6: With reference to the graph you completed in exercise **4-5** -- assuming you created the correct graph -- is it sufficient (i.e., "good enough") that the CS and US occur close together in time for Pavlovian learning to occur? If not, describe what else seems necessary (i.e., "required") for the establishment of a CR. What should we conclude about the necessary and sufficient conditions for a CS to elicit a CR?

4-7: In the graph below, draw the changes in the strength of a CR across 1 session of delay conditioning and 3 sessions of extinction. Be sure to depict spontaneous recovery in the graph.

| Acquisition | Extinction 1 | Extinction 2 | Extinction 3 |

4-8: The British Empiricists were a group of philosophers who tried to identify the principles governing the association of ideas. They noted and hypothesized the following principles:

[1] Ideas occurring together are more strongly associated than those occurring separately.
[2] The more often two ideas occur together, the stronger their association.
[3] The more vivid two ideas are, the stronger their association.

Some contemporary historians and philosophers say that Pavlov's research provides support for the British Empiricists' principles of association.

4-8.1:. Explain this last sentence by describing results from Pavlovian conditioning that correspond to the Empiricists' principles of association. [Hint: Think about temporal contiguity, number of CS-US trials (acquisition), and salience of the CS and US.]

4-8.2:   In separate graphs, illustrate the British Empiricists' 3 principles listed above. [Hint: If you are having some difficulty starting, think about a hypothetical experiment on classical conditioning in which three different researchers separately varied (a) the length of time between the CS and the US, (b) the frequency of CS and US pairings, and (c) the salience of the CS and the US. If you can create a graph that depicts the expected findings from these different manipulations, then you should be able to complete exercise **4-8.2**.]

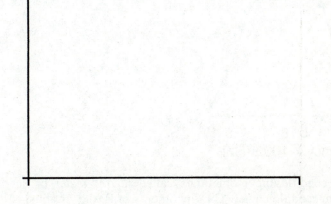

4-8.3:   Which major principle of Pavlovian conditioning is not represented in the principles listed above?   [Hint: Think about the necessary and sufficient conditions for Pavlovian conditioning, and about the concept of "predictiveness" of a CS. Consider also the general ineffectiveness of simultaneous conditioning.]

4-9: Given the data below, describe and explain a *procedure* that likely produced the results? [Hint: you need to *discriminate* among various concepts before you can successfully answer the question.]

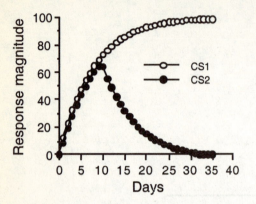

4-10: A person is conditioned to blink to a 6000-Hz tone-CS. The day after the person is blinking during 90% or more of the CS presentations, he is presented with tones of different frequencies. The puff of air is not presented during this test session. The graph below depicts the results of this test day. Which phenomenon of Pavlovian learning is illustrated in the graph? Explain.

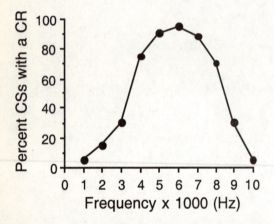

4-11: In higher-order conditioning (sometimes called *second-order* or *secondary* conditioning) an established CS is used to condition a new CS. In other words, the established CS takes on the role of the US. This can be summarized as follows:

Phase 1:   CS1 → US   (e.g., bell followed by food)
Phase 2:   CS2 → CS1 (e.g., light followed by bell)

Eventually, the second CS (the light in our example) comes to elicit a CR similar to the one elicited by the first CS (the bell in our example). Interestingly, it is difficult to produce higher-order conditioning.

> **4-11.1:** Why is it difficult to produce higher-order conditioning?   [Hint: Think about what's happening because the US is not present during Phase 2.]

4-11-2: Given that higher-order conditioning is not easily produced, how is it that, for example, a person who is bitten by a dog might come to fear all sorts of animals? [Hint: The answer might have nothing to do with higher-order conditioning.]

4-12: On December 29, 2001, one of the authors (AM) was in his office at home developing exercises for this workbook. For reasons he cannot remember today, he interrupted his work and headed to the living room. Suddenly, he noticed that something was seriously wrong; he could hear the characteristic crackling of burning wood and the smell of smoke coming from the living room. Upon rushing to the room, he saw that it was filled with thick, black smoke and a sofa was being consumed by an intense fire. The flames reached the ceiling and spread from there in all directions. The temperature was so high and the smoke so thick that he could not get any closer than within 7 ft of the fire. AM panicked: He did not know whether his two children were at home or where he could find the fire extinguisher. Eventually, the neighbors and firefighters came and helped. The fire was eventually extinguished, but not before destroying his living room and causing smoke damage to most of his home and belongings. Due to the amount of smoke he inhaled, AM had to be treated at a local hospital.

During the next few weeks and months, when AM smelled something burning in his home, he became agitated, goose bumps appeared on his skin, his heart pounded, his hands began to sweat, and he had tumultuous thoughts. On most occasions, there was nothing going on; on other occasions, a bit of food was burned as dinner was being prepared. Almost one year after the fire, AM reacts less intensely and less often to false alarms; but, you can still find him occasionally wondering through the house, particularly the kitchen and the adjacent living room, swearing that something is burning.

With reference to various phenomena of Pavlovian conditioning (e.g., conditioned fear, stimulus discrimination and generalization, extinction, etc.), interpret AM's behavior in the few weeks and months following the fire, and also his behavior almost a year later.

5

COMPLEXITIES OF PAVLOVIAN CONDITIONING

Major topics covered in the exercises of this chapter:

Contingency, conditioned inhibition, inhibitors, excitation, excitors, inhibition of delay, conditioned suppression, suppression ratio, external inhibition

Contingency in Pavlovian conditioning

Contingency refers to the extent to which two events are correlated. For example, in Pavlov's original experiment, the tone and food were contingent stimuli because they were correlated. In this case, we can say even more: The contingency was *positive* because the presence of the tone was accompanied by the presence of the food, and the absence of the tone was accompanied by the absence of the food. We may also say that the probability of the US given the presence of the CS was higher than the probability of the US given the absence of the CS.

The contingency between two events may also be *negative*. Suppose Pavlov had done his experiment in the following way: At the end of the tone the dog never received food; in the absence of the tone, that is, during the interstimulus interval, the dog received some food. In this case, the presence of the tone was accompanied by the absence of the food, and the absence of the tone was accompanied by the presence of the food. We could also say that the probability of the US given the presence of the CS was lower than the probability of the US given the absence of the CS.

Conditioned suppression and suppression ratios

Conditioned suppression is measured by a *suppression ratio*, which, as the name implies, is a ratio involving two numbers: [1] the number of responses during the CS and [2] the number of responses during the absence of the CS. By comparing responses in the presence and absence of the CS, we can quantify the effect of the CS. That is, did responding increase, decrease, or remain unchanged during the CS?

Let's examine an example to see how a *suppression ratio* is calculated. You should know by now that when a tone is paired with shock, a well-conditioned rat will press a lever for food less while the tone is on than while the tone is off. Fig 5.1 illustrates this situation. During the first 30 seconds the tone was off and the rat pressed the lever 21 times; let's call this number N_{CS_Off}. During the next 30 seconds, the tone was on and in its presence the rat pressed the lever 5 times; let's call this number N_{CS_On}.

Although there are different ways of calculating a *suppression ratio*, perhaps the most common is to define a suppression ratio as follows:

$$\text{suppression ratio} = N_{CS\_On} / (N_{CS\_On} + N_{CS\_Off})$$

In the example, *suppression ratio* = 5/(5+21) or about 0.19. Now study the ratio for a few minutes. Why do you think the ratio consists of the number of responses while the CS is on divided by the total number of responses while the CS is on *and* off? What is the denominator trying to capture? If you guessed that the denominator consists of the total of all responses, then you guessed right. Thus, the suppression ratio denotes the proportion of responses during the CS relative to all responses made (both in the presence of the CS and in its absence). In this regard, the suppression ratio is like calculating the number of correct responses on a multiple choice exam: The number of correct responses is divided by the number of questions on the exam; that is, by the total number of correct (analogous to the CS_{On}) and incorrect (analogous to the CS_{Off}) questions.[1]

Figure 5.1

How are excitors, inhibitors, and neutral stimuli related to conditioned suppression?

When a stimulus reduces leverpressing (as in the example above), the stimulus is called an *excitor*. The name may sound counterintuitive for, as one student put it: "If the stimulus suppresses responding, then why do we call it an excitor?" The reason the tone is called an excitor is not because it elicits more (or less) responding, but because it is positively correlated with the shock and therefore elicits an observable response that is often similar to the reaction elicited by the shock. In other words, because the tone was paired with the shock (as the bell was paired with food in Pavlov's original experiment), it came to elicit a response similar to that elicited by the shock, which results in a suppression of leverpressing.

Other cases are possible. Imagine that the shock was more likely to occur during the absence than the presence of the tone. In this case, the tone would signal the absence of the shock, a relatively safe period, and in its presence the rat would press the lever more than in its absence. The tone would be called an *inhibitor*. More generally, an inhibitor is stimulus that is negatively correlated with the US and consequently elicits a reaction that is generally opposite to that elicited by the US.[2]

Finally, when tone and shock (or CS and US) are not correlated, either positively or negatively, there is no noticeable difference in the number of leverpresses in the presence and in the absence of the tone. The tone is called *neutral*.

---

[1] An alternative way of defining a suppression ratio is to calculate the number of responses that occurred while the CS was on relative to when it was off (i.e., *suppression ratio* = N_{CS_On} / N_{CS_Off}). In comparison to the other means of defining a suppression ratio, what effect does this alternative formula have on the suppression ratio? Can you think of any situation(s) where this alternative formula for calculating a suppression ratio may be problematic?

[2] It should be noted that detecting inhibitory conditioning is more complicated than detecting excitatory conditioning. For more information about this topic, consult your primary textbook's index and read about *summation tests* and *reacquisition* or *retardation tests*.

EXERCISES

5-1: Let us call $P(US|CS)$ the probability of the US given that the CS is present, and $P(US|No\ CS)$ the probability of the US given that the CS is absent. Based on the examples and definitions of *contingency* provided in the Introduction, complete the following table:

	P(US|CS)	P(US|No CS)	P(US|CS) – P(US|No CS)	Contingency: Positive, Negative, or Neutral?
Case 1	1.0	0.0		
Case 2	0.0	1.0		
Case 3	0.5	0.5		
Case 4	0.7	0.2		
Case 5	0.1	0.4		
Case 6	0.5	0.0		

5-2: Looking at the last two columns of the table, what should you conclude about the sign of the contingency (i.e., whether it is positive or negative) and the difference between the two probabilities $P(US|CS)$ and $P(US|No\ CS)$?

5-3: Suppose that in each of the five cases above, the CS was a tone, the US was food, and the animal was a hungry dog. If we make this supposition, then Case 1 corresponds to Pavlov's original experiment because (a) food always followed the presentation of the tone (i.e., $P(US|CS)=1$) and (b) food was never delivered in the absence of the tone (i.e, $P(US|No\ CS)=0$). In this case, Pavlov reported reliable and strong salivation to the tone.

For each of the other cases, predict whether the tone will excite, inhibit, or not affect salivation and, in the appropriate cases, predict whether the excitation or inhibition will be strong or weak. Explain your predictions.

5-4: Four groups of 10 humans each participated in an eye-blink conditioning experiment. In Group 1, a 0.5-second tone was followed by a puff of air to the eye on every trial (Group 100%); in Groups 2, 3, and 4, the tone was followed by the airpuff on 75%, 50%, and 25% of the trials only. The US never occurred in the absence of the CS (i.e., the US did not occur during the 1-minute intertrial intervals). For each group, the experimenter counted the number of people who blinked to the tone.

In the space below, draw a learning curve for each group and explain your reasoning using the concept of contingency. [Hints: Remember, when plotting a learning curve, you always need to consider two variables -- the rate of learning and the asymptote. Also, you need to take into account two probabilities -- i.e., $P(US|CS)$ and $P(US|No\ CS)$ -- and infer the rates and asymptotes of learning for each group according to the difference between the two probabilities. Finally, you need to determine the dependent and independent variables to plot the learning curves.]

5-5: Using the information about suppression ratios above to assist you, what are the lowest and highest values possible in a *suppression ratio*? [Hint: Discard the possibility that both numbers -- N_{CS_On} and N_{CS_Off} -- are 0, for if this were the case, then there would be nothing to quantify. Mathematically speaking, what makes the ratio increase? What makes it decrease? Consider various numerical combinations for N_{CS_On} and N_{CS_Off}.]

5-6: Given the definitions of *excitors*, *inhibitors*, and *neutral stimuli* presented in the Introduction, determine the minimum and maximum numerical values for the *suppression ratio* in each case below. Enter the values in the table. [Hint: Remember that you are working within a conditioned suppression paradigm.]

The CS is a(n)	Range of Suppression Ratio	
	Minimum	Maximum
Excitor		
Neutral		
Inhibitor		

5-7: Check your understanding of the relationship between *suppression ratios* and whether a CS is an *excitor*, an *inhibitor*, or "associatively" *neutral* by completing the following sentences:

As a stimulus changes from neutral to a strong excitor, the *suppression ratio* changes from

_____ to _____.   The closer the *suppression*

ratio is to _____, the stronger is the excitor.

As a stimulus changes from neutral to a strong inhibitor, the *suppression ratio* changes from

_____ to _____.   The closer the *suppression*

ratio is to _____, the stronger is the inhibitor.

5.8: In one of Pavlov's (1927) experiments, four points were marked in the hind leg of a dog (see points A_1 to A_4 in the figure below). Whenever one of these points was stimulated, the dog received a piece of food.

The training continued until the dog salivated reliably when any of these points was stimulated. Next, Pavlov marked another point in the dog's skin (see point B in the figure), but when he stimulated that point he never gave the dog any food. Pavlov reported the following findings. Initially, the dog salivated when point B was stimulated. However, with additional training the animal ceased to salivate when point B was stimulated. More interestingly, at the end of training, when Pavlov stimulated point B and one of the other four points simultaneously, the animal

[1] did not salivate if the other stimulated point was A_4;
[2] salivated only half of what it used to salivate if the other stimulated point was A_3; and
[3] salivated the usual amount if the other stimulated point was A_1 or A_2.

5-8.1:   Which phenomenon is illustrated by the dog's *initial* response of salivating to B?

5-8.2:   The simultaneous stimulation of point B and one of the A points at the end of training corresponds to a standard testing procedure. Which one? Explain.

5-8.3:   Using the concepts of excitation, conditioned inhibition, and generalization gradient (both for excitation and inhibition), interpret the results of Pavlov's experiment when two points were stimulated.

5-8.4:   Draw a graph to illustrate your interpretation. [Hint: Place the various points A_1 to B along the *x*-axis; draw excitatory and/or inhibitory gradients at the various points; find their net effect.]

5-8: In one of Pavlov's experiments, he observed a mysterious and intriguing phenomenon. First, he conditioned a dog to salivate to an object rotating clockwise by pairing that stimulus with food. Afterwards, he continued to pair that stimulus with food on some of the trials. On the remaining trials, he presented the same-looking object rotating counterclockwise; however, he did not provide food at the end of the trial. In other words, the dog now experienced two types of trials:

[1] Object rotating clockwise → Food
[2] Object rotating counterclockwise → No Food

Pavlov obtained the results summarized in the table below (from Pavlov, 1927):

Day	Time	Stimulus applied during 30 sec	Saliva	Remarks
02/15/1917	3:13 pm	Object rotating clockwise	27	Reinforced
	3:25 pm	Object rotating counterclockwise	7	Not reinforced
02/16/1917	1:04 pm	Object rotating clockwise	24	Reinforced
	1:14 pm	Object rotating clockwise	26	"
	1:25 pm	Object rotating clockwise	27	"
	1:34 pm	Object rotating counterclockwise	10	Not reinforced
02/17/1917	2:45 pm	Object rotating counterclockwise	12	Not reinforced
02/18/1917	2:48 pm	Object rotating clockwise	19	Reinforced
	3:33 pm	Object rotating counterclockwise	34	Not reinforced
02/20/1917	3:07 pm	Object rotating counterclockwise	26	Not reinforced
	3:28 pm	Object rotating clockwise	26	Reinforced
02/21/1917	3:00 pm	Object rotating counterclockwise	12	Not reinforced
Next few days		Object rotating clockwise	26	Reinforced
		Object rotating counterclockwise	0	Not reinforced

Now look at salivation to the object rotating clockwise, the CS+, across presentations. On average, it elicited 25 drops of saliva. Because this stimulus was always reinforced, or paired with the US, Pavlov was not surprised that it elicited copious salivation.

Now look at the salivation to the object rotating counterclockwise, the CS- (a stimulus never reinforced or paired with the US), across presentations. At first, the amount of salivation was small, 7 drops, but it then increased to 34 drops before finally decreasing to 0. Although the counterclockwise stimulus was never reinforced, it elicited increasingly more salivation during its first four presentations, and then increasingly less salivation during its subsequent presentations. Pavlov was intrigued by this change in salivation to the CS-.

Perhaps we can better understand why Pavlov was intrigued if we reason as follows: Initially, the CS+ elicited strong salivation, whereas the CS- did not. This difference in amount of salivation suggests that the dog initially discriminated between the two stimuli. Subsequently, however, both stimuli elicited strong salivation, which suggests that the dog did not discriminate between them. Hmm…. Finally, the dog salivated to the CS+, but not to the CS-, showing that it discriminated the stimuli again. Why would the animal first discriminate, then lose the discrimination, and then discriminate again?

Pavlov solved the mystery by coordinating what he knew about (a) the orientation reflex elicited by new stimuli and the habituation of this reflex, (b) external inhibition, defined as the ability of a novel stimulus to inhibit responding, (c) stimulus generalization, (d) stimulus discrimination, and (e) conditioned inhibition, and found a plausible solution to the mystery.

The challenge for you is to solve *The Mystery of the Counterclockwise Rotating Object* by reconstructing Pavlov's solution. That is, use all five concepts listed above to provide a plausible explanation for why the amount of salivation to the CS- changed over time. [Be patient and persistent! This is a challenging but interesting problem.]

5-9: Pavlov (1927) did an experiment with a dog in which the CS was a mechanical excitation of the skin and the US was an acidic solution in the mouth. The CS lasted for 3 minutes and was then followed by the US. Pavlov measured the number of drops of saliva secreted during the CS.

After several days of training, Pavlov presented the CS alone during two trials and obtained the results shown in the top two rows of the table below. Then, during a test trial, he presented the CS together with a metronome (a new stimulus) and obtained the results shown in the third row of the table. Finally, during two more trials, Pavlov again presented the CS alone and obtained the results shown in the two bottom rows.

Time	Stimulus	Salivary secretion in drops per 30 sec
09:50 a.m.	Tactile	0, 0, 3, 7, 11, 19
10.03 a.m.	Tactile	0, 0, 0, 5, 11, 13
10.15 a.m.	Tactile + metronome	4, 7, 7, 3, 5, 9
10.30 a.m.	Tactile	0, 0, 0, 3, 12, 14
10.50 a.m.	Tactile	0, 0, 5, 10, 17, 19

5-9.1: What type of CS-US arrangement was used during training (i.e., with the tactile stimulus alone)? Explain.

5-9.2: Plot the results in a single graph with 5 curves, and use the graph to answer the remaining questions.

5-9.3: How would you characterize the time course of salivation when the tactile stimulus was presented singly? That is, what is the pattern in the amount of salivation across time?

5-9.4: How would you characterize the results obtained during the third trial (i.e., the tactile + metronome)?

5-9.5: Based on your answer to the preceding questions and noting Pavlov's assumption that inhibition is more easily disrupted than excitation, develop a model to account for the major trends in the data. Here are some ideas:

[1] Assume that you could somehow measure the degrees of excitation and inhibition during the 3-minute presentation of the CS. Excitation would be measured in positive units, inhibition in negative units. To make things simple, assume that excitation is constant throughout the 3-minute interval (as shown in the graph below).

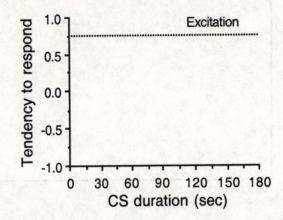

[2] Assume that the CR is proportional to the sum of excitation and inhibition.

[3] From these two assumptions draw one curve -- the time course of inhibition during the 180-sec CS -- such that the sum of the excitation and inhibition curves shows roughly the same trend as, say, the second row of the table.

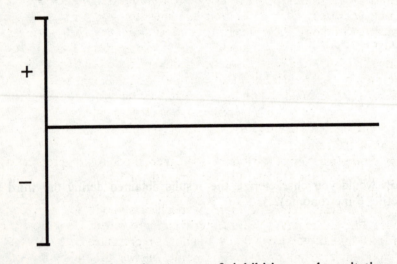

[4] Finally, assume that the curves of inhibition and excitation are reduced proportionately by the new stimulus, but inhibition is disrupted more than excitation. From this extra assumption, derive a trend similar to that in the third row of the table.

6

THE RESCORLA-WAGNER MODEL: THE BASICS

Major topics covered in the exercises of this chapter:

Rescorla-Wagner equation, asymptotes, steady states, salience of CSs, associative strength, applications of the Rescorla-Wagner equation to single CS situations

The Rescorla-Wagner model

The Rescorla-Wagner model attempts to describe what an animal learns about CSs on each trial of a Pavlovian conditioning experiment. The model is based on a set of assumptions concerning CSs, USs, and the learning process. Below, we briefly review these assumptions.

Unconditional Stimulus. Each US is limited in how strongly it can be associated with a CS or, in Rescorla-Wagner terminology, how much *associative strength* it can sustain. Behaviorally, this means that each US is limited in how strong a CR it can sustain. This maximum or *asymptotic* strength, represented below by the letter A, depends on, among other things, the amount or intensity of the US. For example, a certain amount of meat may elicit a maximum of 100 drops of saliva; hence, in this case, $A=100$; a smaller amount of meat may sustain a maximum of only 50 drops, in which case $A=50$. No meat, or more generally no US, corresponds to $A=0$. Note that A is always positive or zero. Some textbook authors use different symbols or letters (e.g., λ instead of A) but the meaning of the term is the same.

Conditional Stimulus. In the Rescorla-Wagner model two properties of each CS are important: [1] the salience of the CS and [2] the strength of its association with the US. Regarding salience, think of it as the attention-grabbing capacity of a CS. A loud sound might be a salient stimulus for a dog and a bright red light might be a salient stimulus for a pigeon. Why is salience important? Because animals generally learn faster with more salient CSs. In the model, the salience of a stimulus is a fixed quantity between 0 and 1 and it is represented below by the letter S.

To check your understanding up to this point, answer the following question: For Fido, a particular tone and light have saliences equal to $S_{Tone}=0.4$ and $S_{Light}=0.1$, respectively. According to the Rescorla-Wagner model, if each stimulus is paired with meat, then Fido will learn to salivate faster to the _____ than to the _____ .

In addition to salience, a CS is characterized also by the strength of its association with the US, which in the Rescorla-Wagner model is often represented by V. To refer to the associations of different stimuli, we use subscripts: V_{Light} and V_{Tone}, or V_1 and V_2, or V_{CS1} and V_{CS2}. These designations are all equivalent. Furthermore, because associations can be positive, negative, or zero the Vs also can be positive, negative or zero. To illustrate the meaning of V, assume that on a particular trial of an experiment with a light, a tone, and a metronome, we have $V_{Light}=20$, $V_{Tone}=-10$, and $V_{Metronome}=0$. This would mean that:

[1]   if the Light were presented alone, then the magnitude of the CR would be 20;

[2]   if the Metronome were presented alone, then the magnitude of the CR would be 0 (i.e., no response would occur);

[3]   if the Tone were presented alone, then the CR would not occur and it would be inhibited by an amount equal to 10. However,

[4]   if two or more stimuli were presented during a trial (e.g., the Light, Metronome, and the Tone), then the magnitude of the CR would be given by the *sum* of their *V*-values. We refer to this sum as V_{Sum}.

Again, to check your understanding, use the *V*-values given above to determine V_{Sum} if the following trials were to take place:

Table 6.1

Stimuli presented during the trial	V_{Sum}
Light + Metronome	
Light + Tone	
Light + Tone + Metronome	
Metronome (Note: Be careful!)	

Let's again check your understanding of what you have learned by now. Circle the term within the parentheses that makes each of the following expressions a true statement:

If $V > 0$, then the CS is a(n) (inhibitor/excitor/neutral stimulus) and it will (elicit/suppress/have no effect on) a CR.

If $V < 0$, then the CS is a(n) (inhibitor/excitor/neutral stimulus) and it will (elicit/suppress/have no effect on) a CR.

If $V = 0$, then the CS is a(n) (inhibitor/excitor/neutral stimulus) and it will (elicit/suppress/have no effect on) a CR.

During an experiment, the salience (*S*) of a CS is a fixed quantity, whereas the strength of the association (*V*) between that stimulus and the US is a variable quantity -- that is, it changes with the animal's experience. This is why *S* is a *parameter* and *V* is a *variable*.

The Learning Process. In the Rescorla-Wagner model, learning is conceived of as a change in the strength of the association (i.e., in the *V*-value) of a CS. We refer to this change as ΔV (read as "delta *V*"). Note that ΔV does not mean "Δ times *V*" or "Δ multiplied by *V*"; it is simply a name for the change in *V* that takes place at the end of each trial. The cornerstone of the model is the equation to compute ΔV:

$$\Delta V_i = S_i \times (A - V_{Sum})$$

On the left side of the equation we have ΔV_i, the amount of change in the strength of the association between stimulus *i* (e.g., a Tone, Light, or Metronome) and the US. On the right-hand side of the equation we have a product of two terms, the salience of stimulus *i* and the difference ($A - V_{Sum}$).

Let's look at this difference more closely:

A is the maximum strength of the CR sustainable by the US presented during a trial;

V_{Sum} is the strength of the CR elicited by the CSs that were present during a trial; and therefore,

$(A - V_{Sum})$ is the difference between the maximum possible response strength given the US used on a particular trial and the actual CR strength elicited by CSs on a particular trial.

Time again to check your understanding. If at any time you experience difficulty understanding what you've read -- the dependent measure for determining this is whether you can answer accurately the "check your understanding" problems -- reread the preceding material and try the "check your understanding" problem again. Once again, circle the term within the parentheses that makes each of the following expressions a true statement:

If A is equal to V_{Sum}, then ΔV_i is (negative/zero/positive) and therefore V_i (decreases/increases/does not change) on a particular trial.

If A is less than V_{Sum}, then ΔV_i is (negative/zero/positive) and therefore V_i (decreases/increases/does not change) on a particular trial.

If A is greater than V_{Sum}, then ΔV_i is (negative/zero/positive) and therefore V_i (decreases/increases/does not change) on a particular trial.

Fig 6.1 should help you apply the Rescorla-Wagner model to a variety of experiments. The flowchart must be used for each trial. As you work with the model, remember the following: **The most common mistake in using the Rescorla-Wagner model is to change the V-value of a stimulus at the end of a trial when that stimulus did not occur during that trial.**

Figure 6.1

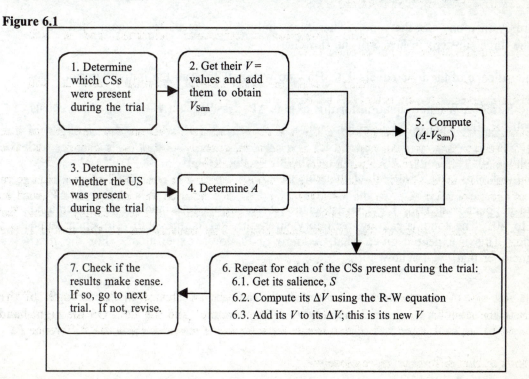

The exercises that follow are divided into two parts. The first part deals with experiments in which there is a single CS; the second part deals with experiments in which there are at least two CSs. When there is only one CS, there is only one V-value. Hence, the subscript for V can be dropped and V_{Sum} is the same as V.

EXERCISES

6-1: Consider Pavlov's basic experiment. On each trial, a dog hears a tone and then receives food. The tone is of moderate intensity, which we represent by a salience parameter equal to $S=0.4$. The amount of food corresponds to $A=100$. Initially, the tone is a neutral stimulus; hence its initial V-value is 0.

> **6-1.1:** Given the preceding description, your task is to complete the table below. To help you get started, we explain how the first row was computed using the 7 steps of the flowchart above.

[1] There was only one CS present, the tone.

[2] The V-value of the tone is initially 0. How do we know? Because this information is given in the experimental description above. Hence, $V_{Tone} = 0$. Because the tone was the only CS, V_{Sum} equals V_{Tone}, that is, 0.

[3] The US was present on the first trial. How do we know? From the description above.

[4] $A=100$. How do we know? Again, from the experimental description.

[5] The difference $(A-V_{Sum})$ equals (100-0), that is, 100.

[6] There is only one CS, the tone. Therefore, only ΔV_{Tone} needs to be computed. We follow the three substeps in box 6 of the flowchart.

[6.1] The salience of the tone equals 0.4. How do we know? From the initial description.

[6.2] The Rescorla-Wagner equation for this case is $\Delta V_{Tone} = S_{Tone} \times (A - V_{Sum})$, which equals $\Delta V_{Tone} = 0.4 \times 100$. That is, $\Delta V_{Tone} = 40$.

[6.3] Adding the V of the tone at the beginning of the trial (i.e., 0) to the ΔV_{Tone} just computed (i.e., 40) gives 0+40=40. This is the new V.

[7] What happened on Trial 1? The association between the tone and the food increased from 0 to 40. The tone is gaining excitatory strength, that is, the ability to elicit some salivation. This is expected given what we know of Pavlov's experiment. For the next trial, remember that V_{Tone} is now 40.

	Trial	Tone?	V_{Sum}	A	ΔV_{Tone}	V_{Tone}
Acquisition	—	—	—	—	—	0
	1	Yes	0	100	40	40
	2					
	3					
	4					
	5					
	6					

6-1.2:   Based on your computations above, label the four quantities (depicted in the figure as question marks) in the figure below. Your options are: ΔV, V, A, and A-V.

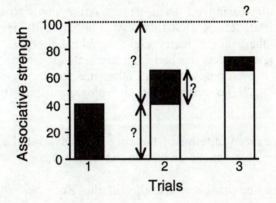

6-1.3:   Plot the values for V_{Tone} in the frame below. However, rather than calculating the values of V_{Tone} for 30 trials, use your knowledge of the Rescorla-Wagner model to extrapolate the curve beyond trial 6.

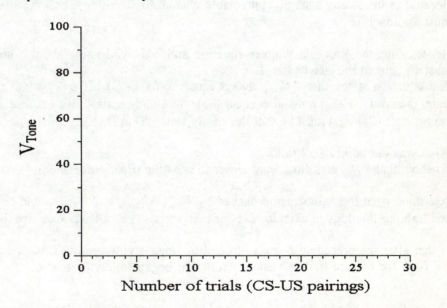

6-1.4:   Suppose that Pavlov had not stopped after trial 6 but continued for many trials, say 1000 or more. Guess what V_{Sum}, ΔV_{Tone}, and V_{Tone} would be. In other words, determine the asymptotic values of these variables. [Hint: If you understand the meaning of these variables, then no calculations are needed to answer this question.]

Do you need a hint? It's worth going through this question piece by piece because if you understand the answers, then you will have understood a great deal about Pavlovian conditioning, the Rescorla-Wagner model, steady states, and transient states.

The first "intellectual leap" you need to make in answering the question is to realize that the *amount* of learning is decreasing on each trial. After many trials, practically no learning occurs following a trial. Think of it this way: You can only learn so much before you've learned everything there is to learn, right? When there is no more learning occurring, then we say that learning has reached a steady state or asymptote. With this in mind, we can now rephrase our original question: What are the steady-state values of the variables V_{Sum}, ΔV_{Tone}, and V_{Tone}? To determine their values, consider the following set of questions and answers:

Q: What does *steady state* mean in terms of learning or behavioral changes?
A: It means that no appreciable change or learning is taking place.

Q: Which quantity represents change or learning in the Rescorla-Wagner model: V_{Tone}, ΔV_{Tone}, A, or S?
A: It is ΔV_{Tone} that stands for *change*, amount, or degree of learning.

Q: Therefore, what must be the value of ΔV_{Tone} at the steady state?
A: Because at the steady state no appreciable change, or learning, is taking place, ΔV_{Tone} must approach 0.

Q: Hence, using the Rescorla-Wagner equation and what you know about S and A, what must V_{Tone} be at the steady state?
A: The equation states that ΔV_{Tone} always equals $S \times (A - V_{Tone})$. If $\Delta V_{Tone}=0$ at the steady state, then $S \times (A - V_{Tone})$ must also equal 0 at the steady state. But because S is not 0, the product $(A - V_{Tone})$ must be 0 at the steady state. That is, V_{Tone} must equal A.

Q: What was the point of all this?
A: To show that V_{Tone} gets closer and closer to A as the trials proceed.

Now, determine what the numbers approached by V_{Sum}, ΔV_{Tone}, and V_{Tone} would be if Pavlov continued training the dogs in exercise **6-1** for many trials (i.e., answer exercise **6-1.4**).

6-2: Assume that after the preceding 6 trials of conditioning, Pavlov removed the food but continued to present the Tone for 6 more trials. That is, extinction began following trial 6.

6-2.1: Given the information in exercises **6-1** and **6-2**, complete the table below:

	Trial	Tone?	V_{Sum}	A	ΔV_{Tone}	V_{Tone}
Extinction	—	—	—	—	—	95.33
	1	Yes				
	2					
	3					
	4					
	5					
	6					

6-2.2: Based on your computations for exercise **6-2.1**, label the three quantities (depicted as question marks) in the figure below. Your options are: ΔV, V, and A

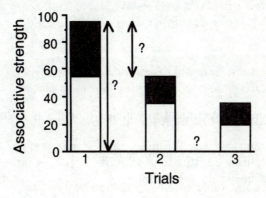

6-2.3: Why was the term A-V not included as an option?

6-2.4: What are the steady-state values of the variables V_{Sum}, ΔV_{Tone}, and V_{Tone}?

6-2.5: Use the Rescorla-Wagner equation to prove your answers to exercise **6-2.4**. Need some hints? Try answering the following questions:

Q: What does *steady state* mean in terms of learning or behavioral changes?
A:

Q: Which quantity represents change or learning in the Rescorla-Wagner model?

A:

Q: Therefore, what must be the value of ΔV_{Tone} at the steady state?

A:

Q: Hence, using the Rescorla-Wagner equation and what you know about S and A, what must V_{Tone} be at the steady state?

A:

6-3: Consider a Pavlovian conditioning experiment in which a tone-CS is followed by a food-US.

6-3.1: Compute the first ten V-values assuming that V starts at 0, S=0.1, and A=100. Repeat your computations but this time take S=0.4 (i.e., a more intense stimulus is used). Enter your values in the tables below.

S=0.1	Trial	V_{Sum}	A	ΔV_{Tone}	V_{Tone}
	—	—	—	—	0
	1	0	100		
	2				
	3				
	4				
	5				
	6				
	7				
	8				
	9				
	10				

S=0.4	Trial	V_{Sum}	A	ΔV_{Tone}	V_{Tone}
	—	—	—	—	0
	1	0	100		
	2				
	3				
	4				
	5				
	6				
	7				
	8				
	9				
	10				

6-3.2: Plot your two sets of results for V_{Tone} on the same graph and interpret them. Be sure to explain the effect of changing S.

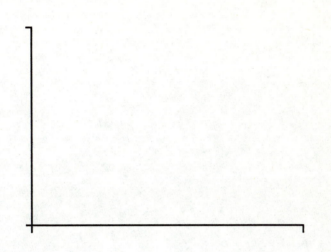

6-3.3: Using the Rescorla-Wagner equation and the concept of steady state, prove that the long-term, steady-state value of V does not depend on S.

7

THE RESCORLA-WAGNER MODEL: ADVANCED ISSUES

Major topics covered in the exercises of this chapter:

Applications of the Rescorla-Wagner equation to overshadowing, blocking, conditioned inhibition

Introduction

Whereas the previous chapter dealt with how the Rescorla-Wagner model handled acquisition and extinction in Pavlovian conditioning situations with a single CS and US, this chapter covers more advanced uses of the Rescorla-Wagner model. We note again that although some students find the material in the previous chapter and this one difficult, it is worth investing the effort to learn how to use the model and, most importantly, the meaning of its various terms and how they relate to learning (a transient state) and asymptotic behavior (a steady state).

In this chapter we use the Rescorla-Wagner model to describe and predict multi-CS situations. Remember, when there are two or more CSs, the Rescorla-Wagner equation must be used for each CS present during a trial. Thus, if on a trial a light and tone were presented, we would need to compute separately ΔV_{Tone} and ΔV_{Light}. Moreover, a stimulus *must* be present during a trial for its V-value to change. If stimulus i is absent during a trial, then its V-value does not change on that trial and therefore $\Delta V_i = 0$.

EXERCISES

7-1: The table below describes an experiment with 3 groups of rats. The uppercase CR means that a CS elicited a strong conditioned response; the lowercase cr means that a CS elicited a weak conditioned response.

7-1.1: What phenomenon of Pavlovian conditioning is illustrated by the results in the table?

	Training Phase	Results
Group A	CS1+CS2→US	CS1→CR; CS2→cr
Group B	CS1→US	CS1→CR
Group C	CS2→US	CS2→CR

7-1.2: The Rescorla-Wagner model accounts for this phenomenon by assuming that the salience of CS1 is greater than the salience of CS2. To better understand the account, assume that $S_{CS1}=0.2$ and $S_{CS2}=0.1$ and then complete the table below, which refers to Group A.

Trial	CS1	CS2	A	V_{Sum}	ΔV_{CS1}	ΔV_{CS2}	V_{CS1}	V_{CS2}
—	—	—	—	—	—	—	0	0
1								
2								
3								
4								
5								
6								
7								
8								
9								
10								
Steady state								

7-2: Consider the result of the following experiment. During the first 20 days, one group of rats is trained using the conditioned suppression paradigm -- i.e., a tone is followed by shock until the tone reliably reduces the rat's rate of leverpressing for food. During the next 10 days, the experimenter presents the same tone with a light and then the shock. Finally, during a test phase, the experimenter presents the tone alone on some trials and the light alone on another trials. In both cases, the experimenter measures the rat's rate of leverpressing. What is the result of the experiment?

7-3: The table below describes an experiment similar to the one in exercise **7-2**, except that the conditioned suppression paradigm is not used. The dash (--) in Group A's results means that a CS did not elicit any conditional response.

7-3.1: What important phenomenon of Pavlovian conditioning is illustrated in the table below?

	Phase 1	Phase 2	Results
Group A	CS1→US	CS1+CS2→US	CS1→CR; CS2→ --
Group B		CS1+CS2→US	CS1→CR; CS2→ CR

7-3.2: After filling in the two tables below for Group A, explain how the Rescorla-Wagner model accounts for this phenomenon ($S_{CS1}=S_{CS2}=0.2$). Note: The steady state value for V_{CS1} at the end of Phase 1 is equal to the first value of V_{CS1} at the beginning of Phase 2.

Phase 1

Trial	CS1	A	V_{Sum}	ΔV_{CS1}	V_{CS1}
—	—	—	—	—	0
1					
2					
3					
4					
5					
Steady state					

Phase 2

Trial	CS1	CS2	A	V_{Sum}	ΔV_{CS1}	ΔV_{CS2}	V_{CS1}	V_{CS2}
—	—	—	—	—	—	—	—	0
1								
2								
3								
4								
5								
Steady state								

7-4: Imagine that when your uncle and aunt visit, you always find $100 in your desk after they leave. Your uncle sometimes visits alone (i.e., without your aunt), and on these days you also find $100 in your desk after he leaves. Your aunt, however, has never visited alone (i.e., without your uncle).

7-4.1: How much money would you expect to find in your desk if one day in the future (a) your uncle visited alone and, for the first time, (b) your aunt visited alone. After you answer this question, keep this hypothetical situation in mind as you work through exercise **7-5**.

7-5: On odd-numbered trials, two stimuli (a tone and a light) are presented and followed by the US. On even-numbered trials, the tone is presented and followed by the US.

7-5.1:   Complete the table below, assuming the following initial values: V_{Tone} and $V_{Light}=0$, both with salience equal to 0.1. A "1" in the Tone and Light columns means that the stimulus was presented; a "0" means that the stimulus was absent.

Trial	Tone	Light	A	V_{Sum}	ΔV_{Tone}	ΔV_{Light}	V_{Tone}	V_{Light}
—	—	—	—	—	—	—	0	0
1	1	1	100					
2	1	0	100					
3	1	1	100					
4	1	0	100					
5								
6								
7								
8								
9								
10								
11								
12								
13								
14								
15								
16								
17								
18								
19								
20								

7-5.2:   Plot the two sets of *V*-values in a graph.

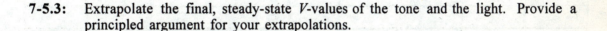

7-5.3: Extrapolate the final, steady-state *V*-values of the tone and the light. Provide a principled argument for your extrapolations.

7-6: Imagine now a slightly different situation: When your uncle and aunt visit, you always find $100 in your desk after they leave. When your uncle visits alone, however, you find no money in your desk after he leaves. Your aunt has never visited alone. Would you expect to see $100 in your desk if one day you saw (a) your uncle alone at the door, and, (b) on another day, your aunt alone at the door? Think about this hypothetical situation as you work through the next problem.

7-7: As before, on odd-numbered trials, a tone and a light are presented and followed by the US. On even-numbered trials, however, the tone is presented but it is *not* followed by the US.

7-7.1: Complete the table below, assuming the following initial values: V_{Tone} and $V_{Light}=0$, both with salience equal to 0.1.

Trial	Tone	Light	A	V_{Sum}	ΔV_{Tone}	ΔV_{Light}	V_{Tone}	V_{Light}
—	—	—	—	—	—	—	0	0
1	1	1	100					
2	1	0	0					
3	1	1	100					
4	1	0	0					
5								
6								
7								
8								
9								
10								
11								
12								
13								
14								
15								
16								
17								
18								
19								
20								

7-7.2: Plot the two sets of V-values in a graph.

7-7.3:   Extrapolate the final, steady-state V-values of the tone and the light. Provide a principled argument for your extrapolations.

7-8: Explain what is surprising about the results you obtained in exercises **7-5** and **7-7**. [Hint: Look at how the light was treated in the two experiments, or how your aunt treated you in the two hypothetical situations, and then look at the steady-state value of the light in each case.]

7-9: Remember what you have learned about conditioned inhibition and then circle the correct term within the parentheses. If a CS signals the (absence/presence) of the US in a context where the US is expected to occur, then the CS will become a/n (excitor/inhibitor/neutral stimulus).

7-10: A Pavlovian conditioning experiment with a dog was divided into two phases. During Phase 1 a tone (CS1) was paired on each trial with two pieces of food (US). At the steady state, the tone elicited strong salivation. Next, during Phase 2, the same tone (CS1) was presented together with a light (CS2) and then *one* piece of food was given to the dog. The pairings CS1+CS2→US occurred for many trials.

7-10.1:   Predict the results of the experiment by stating what the animal will do when each stimulus is presented separately at the end of Phase 2. Be sure to explain your answer.

7-10.2:   How could you test your explanation of the animal's response to the CS2?

7-10.3: Complete the following table, which refers to Phase 1. Assume these initial conditions: $A=200$; $S_{Tone}=0.2$; $V_{Tone}=0$.

Phase 1

Trial	CS1	*A*	V_{Sum}	ΔV_{CS1}	V_{CS1}
—	—	—	—	—	0
1					
2					
3					
4					
5					
6					
Steady state					

7-10.4: The table below pertains to Phase 2. Complete the table, assuming these initial conditions: $A=100$; $S_{Light}=0.2$; $V_{Light}=0$. [Hint: To predict the steady-state *V*-values of the tone, it might help to draw a stylized, but clear, graph of the *V*-values.]

Phase 2

Trial	CS1	CS2	*A*	V_{Sum}	ΔV_{CS1}	ΔV_{CS2}	V_{CS1}	V_{CS2}
—	—	—	—	—	—	—		0
1								
2								
3								
4								
5								
6								
Steady state								

7-10.5: Explain why the asymptotic, steady-state *V*-values of the two stimuli at the end of Phase 2 are what you predicted.

7-11: *Note: This example is different from the ones in exercises 7-4 and 7-6.*   Imagine that when Uncle Sam visits, he always puts a $100 bill on your desk before he leaves.   However, when Aunt Mary comes along with him, you find no money on your desk afterwards.

> **7-11.1:** After these events occur many times, would you predict any money when (a) you see Uncle Sam *alone* at the door, and (b) when you see Aunt Mary *alone* at the door?

> **7-11.2:** Which phenomenon of Pavlovian conditioning does the example illustrate? Explain.

7-12: Assume that during the first phase of an experiment, the *V*-value of a tone, V_T, reached 90. During the second phase of the experiment, a new stimulus, a light, with initial *V*-value equal to zero (i.e., $V_L=0$), was presented with the tone but no food was delivered (extinction).   The tone and light have the same salience, $S_T=S_L=0.2$.

> **7-12.1:** Predict the values of V_T and V_L at the steady state.

Having trouble? A few hints might be helpful. Try answering the following questions:

[1]   What must be true of $V_{Sum}= V_L+V_T$ at the steady state?

[2]   Given the same saliences, what is always true about ΔV_L and ΔV_T during each extinction trial?

[3]   From your answer to [2] and knowing that the initial *V*-values were $V_T=90$ and $V_L=0$, write a second equation relating V_L and V_T.

[4]   Solve the equation and find V_L and V_T.

8

REINFORCEMENT

Major topics covered in the exercises of this chapter:

Amount and quality of reinforcement, motivation, delay of reinforcement, Premack's principle, response deprivation hypothesis, bliss points

Amount and quality of reinforcement

As in Pavlovian conditioning, there are several variables that affect how quickly an operant response is learned and the steady-state (i.e., final or asymptotic) level of performance. The amount and quality of reinforcement are two of these variables. In general, larger reinforcers support more behavior, such as when rats will run faster down an alley-maze to obtain 1 gram of food than to obtain 0.05 grams of food. Similarly, reinforcers of "better" quality support more behavior than those of lower quality. For example, rats will press a lever more rapidly for a solution of sucrose rather than saccharin.

Motivation

An animal's motivational state, such as how hungry or thirsty it is, also influences the effectiveness of a reinforcer. For example, rats deprived of food for 22 hours will run down an alley-maze faster than rats deprived of food for 4 hours. In addition, the rats that are more food-deprived will also reach their asymptotic speed faster than the rats that are less food-deprived.

Delay of reinforcement

Just as contiguity between a CS and US is important for Pavlovian conditioning, so too is contiguity between a response and a reinforcer important for operant conditioning. In general, a reinforcer that immediately follows a response is more effective than a reinforcer that follows a response after a delay.

Premack's principle

As your textbook probably describes, a matter of great contention for more than half a century has been what makes something a reinforcer, or, more casually speaking, what makes a reinforcer reinforcing. The issue is still unresolved, though there is evidence suggesting that some form of behavioral equilibrium may underlie what makes something a reinforcer.

According to Premack's principle, it is perhaps more straightforward to conceive of reinforcers as responses rather than stimuli (i.e., think of drinking instead of water, and eating instead of food). In Premack's view, each behavior has a probability of occurrence during baseline, which we can measure either by the number of times the behavior occurs or by the total time (duration) taken by that behavior. After we measure the probabilities of the behaviors during baseline, we can rank-order them from the most probable to the least probable. Premack's principle states that a more probable behavior will reinforce a less probable behavior if the less probable behavior is followed by the more probable behavior. If this sounds a bit confusing, consider the following:

1. During baseline it was found that Behavior B was more probable than Behavior A.
2. Then, if during an experiment B follows A (i.e., A→B), then A will be reinforced.

To illustrate the principle, suppose a rat took more time eating than leverpressing during baseline (this might occur because the animal was food deprived for 24 hours, for example). Eating would be considered the more probable behavior and leverpressing the less probable behavior. According to Premack's principle, in this case eating would reinforce leverpressing if eating followed leverpressing. In other words, if during an experiment pressing the lever was followed by eating, then the frequency or duration of leverpressing would increase above its baseline levels.

Response deprivation hypothesis

Although Premack's principle accounts well for a relatively large set of findings, it does not explain why in some circumstances a less probable behavior can reinforce a more probable behavior. For example, doing math can reinforce writing even if a child spends much more time writing than doing math. How can this happen?

According to the *response deprivation hypothesis* (sometimes also known as *response disequilibrium*), the opportunity to engage in any behavior that occurs at some level greater than zero during baseline can be used to reinforce any other behavior. For that to happen, the reinforcing behavior must be below its baseline level or, to say it in other words, the subject must be deprived of the reinforcing behavior. In relation to the example above, the opportunity to do math can reinforce writing if doing math is below its baseline level (i.e., has been restricted).

Behavioral bliss points

An extension of the response deprivation hypothesis concerns the idea of *behavioral bliss points*. This view assumes that animals distribute their behavior among available alternatives in a way that is "optimal" for them. Fig 8.1 shows the bliss point for two responses: leverpressing and running. In actuality, the bliss point applies to all of an animal's responses.

Figure 8.1

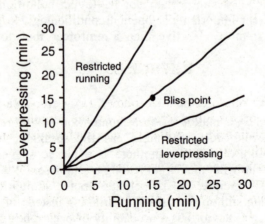

As can be seen in the figure, in this particular case the bliss point corresponds to 15 minutes of leverpressing and 15 minutes of running. That is, during baseline, this rat will spend as much time running as leverpressing -- 15 minutes in both cases.

Now let's see how imposing a contingency between leverpressing and running disrupts the bliss point. Let's first consider a situation in which *x* amount of running is required for *x* amount of leverpressing. This 1:1 relation between leverpressing and running is depicted by the line that passes through the bliss point. In this situation, the animal can satisfy the contingency *and* reach its bliss point.

Let's next consider a situation in which leverpressing is restricted. As depicted on the graph, the imposed contingency requires the animal to run twice as much before it is allowed to press the lever. With this contingency, no distribution of responding will allow the animal to achieve its bliss point. The same is true if running is restricted.

The question is: What does an animal do when a contingency prevents it from reaching its bliss point? According to some studies, the animal will distribute its behavior in such a way that it comes as close as possible to its bliss point. Fig 8.2 illustrates how this works.

Figure 8.2

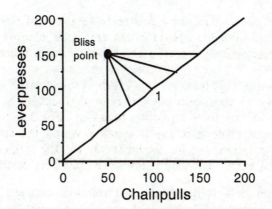

In this figure, the rat's bliss point consists of 150 instances of leverpressing and 50 instances of pulling a chain suspended from the ceiling of an operant chamber, a 3:1 ratio. However, the experimenter has imposed a contingency that requires equal amounts of chainpulling and leverpressing. Thus, for example, for every pull of the chain, the rat will be allowed to press the lever once, a 1:1 ratio. Under this contingency, the rat cannot reach its bliss point (Why?). What does the rat do? The rat distributes its behavior in such a way that it comes as close as possible to its bliss point. From the graph above, line 1 is the point on the contingency line that is closest to the bliss point; therefore, over time, the rat will pull the chain 100 times to be allowed to press the lever 100 times.

EXERCISES

8-1: Psychologists define positive reinforcement as follows: (a) A response-dependent consequence is presented, (b) the response then occurs more often, and (c) the response occurs more often because of the response-consequence relationship. Although nonpsychologists are generally aware of the first two points, they often overlook the third.

To see the relevance of this last point, consider the following example: A little boy is engaging in a temper tantrum that consists of, among other responses, crying and yelling. In an attempt to stop the tantrum, the father shouts "STOP IT!" However, the result of the father's behavior is that the child cries and yells even more, which leads the father to again shout "STOP IT!" A nonpsychologist reasons that shouting "STOP IT!" was a consequence of crying and yelling, so point (a) of the definition described above is satisfied. The responses, crying and yelling, then occurred more often, so point (b) is also satisfied. The nonpsychologist thus concluded that shouting "STOP IT!" functioned as a positive reinforcer for crying and yelling.

8-1.1:   What, if anything is wrong with the nonpsychologist's reasoning?

8-1.2:   Design an experiment that would show whether a stimulus is a positive reinforcer. Pay particular attention to what conditions are necessary to show that a stimulus is a positive reinforcer.

8-2: Larger reinforcers generally produce more or "higher" levels of behavior.

8-2.1:   Draw a graph that depicts the functional relation between the speed that rats traverse a maze (measured in cm/sec) and the amount of reinforcement they receive for doing so.

8-2.2:   Draw a graph that depicts the functional relation between the speed that rats traverse a maze and the amount of reinforcement they receive for doing so. However, in this case, speed is operationally defined as how long (in sec) it takes the rat to reach the end of the maze.

8-2.3:   Examine the graphs you drew for exercises **8-2.1** and **8-2.2**. How is it that the same independent variable (amount of reinforcement) seems to produce different effects?

8-3: Larger reinforcers also tend to produce higher levels of asymptotic (steady-state) responding. Depict this effect on a single graph with two curves by drawing how many math problems (i.e., the y-axis) a group of children solve across days (i.e., the x-axis) when they are given 2 points for completing a problem (one curve) versus another group of children given 1 point for each problem (the second curve).

8-4: Interpret the following graph that compares how fast a monkey presses a lever for M&M peanuts versus plain peanuts. In your answer, be sure to state what you conclude about the "reinforcing value" of the two types of peanuts.

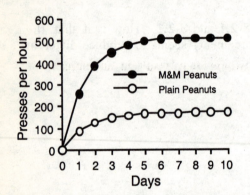

8-5: Interpret the following graph that depicts the number of leverpresses when a press is immediately followed by food reinforcement and when a press is followed by food reinforcement after a 2-sec delay. Be sure to state your conclusion about the role of contiguity between a response and a reinforcer.

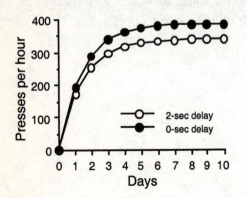

8-6: Using their common sense, many parents often tell their kids that they can watch television only after they do their homework. Is there science underlying parents' common sense? Explain.

8-7: Consider an experiment in which a wine connoisseur's baseline level of drinking two types of wines is as follows: In the observation period, the connoisseur took 6 sips of a sweet dessert wine and 4 sips of a dry white wine. Then, as part of this experiment, this person's access to sweet dessert wine was restricted such that he had to sip the dry wine before he was given access to the sweet wine.

8-7.1:   Distinguish between Premack's principle and the response deprivation hypothesis.

8-7.2:   According to Premack's principle, will this arrangement result in an increase in sipping dry wine? Explain.

8-7.3:   In the next phase of the experiment, the connoisseur was required to take 10 sips of the sweet wine for 1 sip of the dry wine. According to Premack's principle, will this arrangement result in an increase in drinking sweet wine? Explain.

8-7.4:   According to the response deprivation hypothesis, will the arrangement in exercise **8-7.3** be successful? Explain and illustrate your answer with a graph.

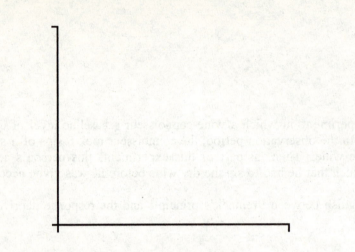

8-8: Look at the two graphs below. After finding the rat's baseline or bliss point (filled circle), the researchers imposed a contingency between the two activities. The contingencies are depicted by the diagonal lines on the graph. As shown in the left panel, the contingency required that the rat spend 3 units of time running before it could drink for one unit of time. Hence, once the rat decided, so to speak, how much time to spend running (let's call this time, y), the amount of time to spend drinking (let's call this time, x) was set and equaled $y/3$. The right panel is similar except that the activities are interchanged. Under this contingency, the experimenter recorded the amount of time the rats engaged in each activity.

8-8.1:   On the graphs below, draw two lines from each bliss point to the contingency line such that one of the lines you draw meets the contingency line at a point consistent with Premack's Principle and the other line at a point inconsistent with it.

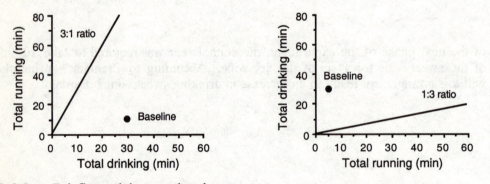

8-8.2:   Briefly explain your drawings.

8-9: The graph below shows the baseline or bliss point for one animal's behavioral distribution and the contingency imposed by a researcher (the diagonal line). During baseline, the animal spends 25 minutes drinking and 15 minutes running. However, the contingency forces the animal to deviate from its bliss point and to distribute its behavior in such a way that it satisfies the contingency (i.e., falls on the contingency line). Note that the contingency does not force the animal to stay at any specific point on the line. Why? Because the contingency allows the animal to engage in one behavior, say running, only after it engages in drinking for a certain amount of time. Similarly, the experimenter allows the animal to engage in drinking only after it engaged in running for a certain amount of time. As depicted in the graph, the ratio of drinking to running is 4:1.

8-9.1: Given that the animal wants to be at baseline (the bliss point) but the contingency requires it to deviate from baseline, how will the animal redistribute its behavior? That is, draw the point on the contingency line that illustrates how the animal will distribute its behavior to meet the contingency.

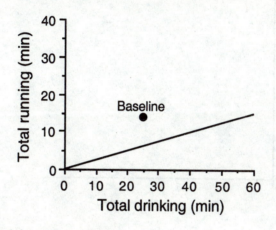

8-9.2: Briefly explain your answer.

8-9.3: Compare your answer to Premack's principle, the response deprivation hypothesis, and a bliss points analysis of response distribution. Which, if any, is most consistent with your answer? Explain.

8-10: Consider the following example: A child's bliss point for prosocial behavior to parental rewards is 1:11, which means that the child prefers to perform one prosocial behavior for every 11 parental rewards. Unsatisfied with this ratio, the parents implement a contingency that requires 1 prosocial behavior to produce 2 parental rewards. Still dissatisfied with the new level of prosocial behavior, the parents implement a new contingency that requires 1 prosocial behavior for 1 parental reward. However, when they implemented this new contingency, the number of prosocial behaviors decreased below the level established when 1 prosocial behavior produced 2 parental rewards.

In the space below, draw a plausible graph to illustrate why prosocial behavior decreased during the new contingency. Include in your graph: (a) the bliss point, (b) a line for the initial contingency, (c) the equilibrium point for this contingency, (d) a second line for the new contingency, and (d) the equilibrium point for the new contingency. As always, be sure to label your graphs.

9

"CREATING" BEHAVIOR: SHAPING

Major topics covered in the exercises of this chapter:

Shaping, successive approximations, behavioral selection, behavioral variation, hot-and-cold game, criterion responses

Shaping

Shaping is a *procedure* used to establish new behavior, that is, behavior not presently performed by an individual or which has an almost zero probability of occurring spontaneously. For example, without explicit training it is unlikely that a dog will catch and retrieve a Frisbee, a child will utter a sentence with more than one word, or an inexperienced surfer will ride a large wave to the shore.

Successive approximations

Shaping is also known as the *method of successive approximations* because it involves (a) the reinforcement of responses that come successively closer to a target behavior, and (b) the extinction of behaviors that are further away from the target behavior. The reinforcer can be controlled by an experimenter, therapist, coach, parent, or by Mother Nature, as in the surfing example above. Let's consider a detailed example of training a rat to rear and pull a string.

A student is trying to shape a rat to stand on its hind legs and pull with its forepaws a string suspended from the ceiling of an experimental chamber. The response of rearing anywhere in the chamber was selected as the first approximation to the target behavior. After a few reinforcers, the rat was readily rearing at various locations in the chamber. As a second step, the rat was reinforced for orienting toward the string. After a few more reinforcers, the rat frequently looked at the string. As a third approximation, the rat was reinforced only if it approached the area underneath the string. This goal also was attained. In the next step, the rat was reinforced only if it reared and touched the string. Once this response was occurring reliably, the rat was reinforced only when it reared and pulled the string. After a few reinforcers, the rat was reliably engaging in the target behavior. Thus, shaping the rat to pull the string could be summarized as follows:

1st Approximation
> *Goal*: Increase rearing
> *Reinforce*: Rearing regardless of where it occurs in the chamber
> *Extinguish*: All responses that do not involve rearing

2nd Approximation
> *Goal*: Increase rearing in the vicinity of the string
> *Reinforce*: The subset of rearing responses that occur near the string
> *Extinguish*: Rearing in other locations

3rd Approximation
   Goal: Increase touching the string
   Reinforce: Touching the string with the forepaws
   Extinguish: Rearing without touching the string

4th Approximation
   Goal: Increase pulling the string
   Reinforce: Pulling the string with the forepaws
   Extinguish: All other responses

Interplay between reinforcement and extinction

Although widely used by animal trainers, moms and dads, teachers and therapists, friends and foes, there is relatively little systematic research on shaping and, thus, relatively few known properties of the procedure. It is known that frequent reinforcement is necessary to keep the animal active and thereby increase the probability of it emitting a closer approximation to the target behavior, but too much reinforcement for a response can lead to the persistence of that response and a slowing down of the training. In these circumstances, it is necessary to reduce the frequency of reinforcement, but at the risk of inactivity and the extinction of previously established responses. You can see that shaping requires a fine balance between reinforcement and extinction. Reinforcement motivates the subject and strengthens appropriate behavior, whereas extinction weakens inappropriate behavior and motivates the subject to try new responses.

EXERCISES

9-1: Describe the *role* of each of the following during shaping:

   9-1.1:   successive approximations

   9-1.2:   reinforcement

   9-1.3:   extinction

   9-1.4:   behavioral variation

9-2: The purpose of this exercise is to help you visualize how behavior is redistributed as a result of different criteria for reinforcement. To illustrate, consider the graph below, which shows the percentage of time a rat spent at different distances from a string suspended from the ceiling of an experimental chamber. The target behavior is to contact the string.

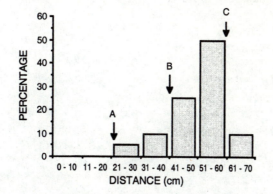

9-2.1: What percentage of the rat's behavior (time spent at different distances) will be *extinguished* if the criterion for the initial approximation is set to position A shown in the graph? Position B? Position C?

9-2.2: What percentage of the rat's behavior will be *reinforced* if the criterion for the initial approximation is set to position A? Position B? Position C?

9-2.3: How are the answers to exercises **9-2.1** and **9-2.2** related to the observation that frequent reinforcement is necessary to keep an animal active (thereby increasing the probability of a closer approximation to the target behavior), but too much reinforcement for a response can lead to the persistence of that behavioral approximation?

9-3: The purpose of this exercise is to further help you visualize and understand how behavior changes as a result of shaping.

9-3.1: In the space below, draw a plausible frequency distribution of the cadence of someone who speaks very rapidly.

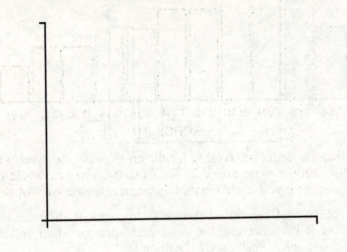

9-3.2: Draw a new frequency distribution that illustrates how the cadence could be changed as a result of shaping. In your graph, indicate which cadences were reinforced and which were not.

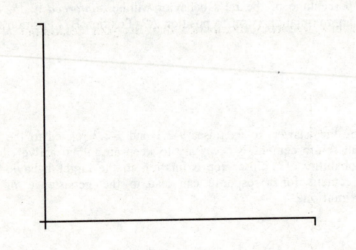

9-4: The purpose of this exercise is to illustrate how extreme forms of behavior can be eliminated through shaping. The graph at the top of the next page shows a frequency distribution of how much force a rat uses to press a lever for food.

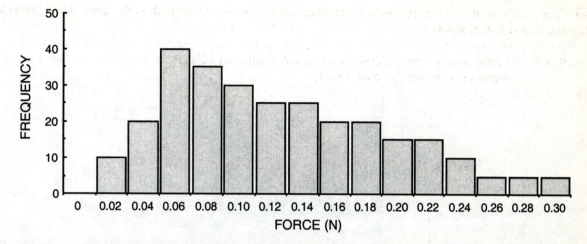

9-4.1:   Assume that the target behavior is for the rat to press the lever with a force of at least 0.10 N but not more than 0.20 N. Describe how you would shape this target response, and how you could obtain this target response without shaping.

9-4.2:   Draw a new frequency distribution that fits your description of the final target behavior.

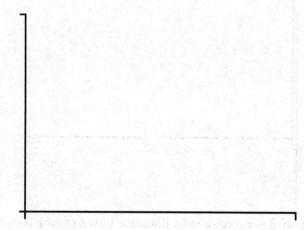

9-5: The purpose of this exercise is to illustrate how shaping can be used to promote behavioral variation. The graph below shows the distribution of the amount of different-colored paints used by an aspiring artist. An aspect of being a successful artist requires that one's work be sufficiently novel from one's previous work.

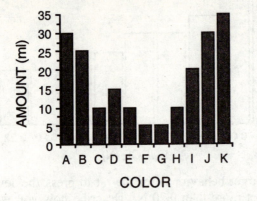

9-5.1:   Describe how you could use shaping to change the aspiring artist's use of colors so that his paintings are more variable.

9-5.2:   What reinforcer(s) might you use? Explain your reasoning.

9-5.3:   Draw a new frequency distribution that fits your description of how his use of color is changing.

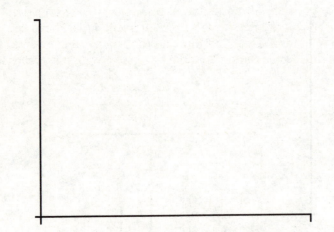

9-6: The hot-and-cold game, in which an instructor "shapes" a student's behavior by saying *hot* and *cold* when the student gets closer to or farther from, respectively, emitting the target response, is not a good example of shaping. One potential problem is that saying *hot* is not an instance of reinforcement nor saying *cold* is an instance of extinction. Instead, these are instances of reinforcement and punishment; remaining silent when a student is getting farther from the target behavior is an instance of extinction. Second, the person saying *hot* and *cold* often dispenses these reinforcers and punishers in a series of gradations by saying *hot, hotter, very hot,* or *cold, colder, very cold.*

   9-6.1:   How might these two differences between the hot-and-cold game and shaping affect a subject's behavior during the game?

   9-6.2:   Design an experiment to test which is better for conditioning rats to leverpress: shaping or the (rat equivalent of the) hot-and-cold game.

9-7: The purpose of this exercise is to help you further identify variables that might be important for shaping. Let's begin by considering the histogram below, which shows an abstract representation of the probability of an organism emitting different responses. The vertical mark separating the two horizontal arrows illustrates where the criterion for reinforcement has been set. The bars of different shades represent behavior to either side of the criterion. In other words, the two sets of bars correspond to the probabilities of emitting "correct" or above-criterion responses and "incorrect" or below-criterion responses.

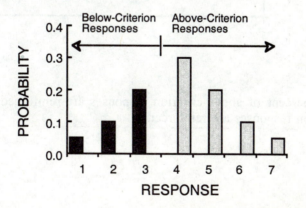

9-7.1:   Assuming that every above-criterion response is reinforced, what is the probability of a reinforced response?   Similarly, if every below-criterion response is extinguished, what is the probability of a nonreinforced response?

9-7.2:   In the preceding question, we assumed that every above-criterion response was reinforced and that every below-criterion response was never reinforced. However, it is possible to reinforce only some of the above-criterion responses, and to occasionally reinforce below-criterion responses.   Using the histogram above as the starting point, draw a plausible histogram which shows the probability of emitting above-criterion and below-criterion responses for each of the following scenarios:

[1]   Seventy-five percent of above-criterion responses are reinforced (meaning that 25% of above-criterion responses are unreinforced) and below-criterion responses are never reinforced;

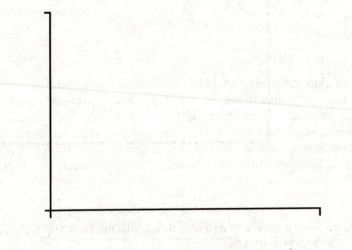

[2]   Fifty percent of above-criterion responses are reinforced and 50% of below-criterion responses are reinforced;

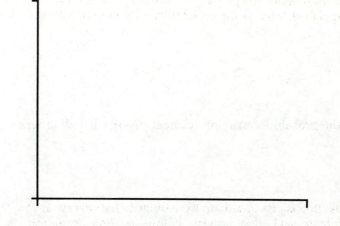

[3] Twenty-five percent of above-criterion responses are reinforced and 75% of below-criterion responses are reinforced.

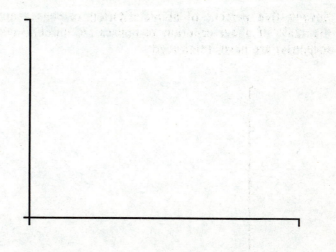

9-7.3:   Based up your answers to exercise **9-7.2**, discuss how the following variables might affect the shaping process:

[1] changes in the criterion for reinforcement;

[2] the probability of reinforcement *given* an above-criterion response;

[3] the probability of reinforcement *given* a below-criterion response.

9-7.4: In addition to the variables discussed in exercise **9-7.3**, briefly describe one other variable that might affect shaping.

10

SCHEDULES OF REINFORCEMENT

Major topics covered in the exercises of this chapter:

Schedules of reinforcement, variable-interval schedule, fixed-interval schedule, variable-ratio schedule, fixed-ratio schedule, cumulative records, feedback functions, partial reinforcement extinction effect (PREE), superstition

What are schedules of reinforcement?

A *schedule of reinforcement* is a rule that specifies the conditions under which a consequence, usually a reinforcer, will occur. In operant conditioning, this usually requires specifying the stimulus conditions and response(s) necessary to produce a consequence. Sometimes the schedules are relatively simple, such as when a rat receives food reinforcement each time it presses a lever. This types of schedule is known as *continuous reinforcement* (abbreviated CRF) or a *fixed-ratio* 1 (abbreviated FR 1). Other times, the schedule can be more complex, such as when a rat receives food after two leverpresses if and only if a light above the lever is green; leverpresses while the light is any other color have no effect.

The importance of schedules of reinforcement

To begin understanding the importance of schedules of reinforcement, consider the following series of thought questions:

1. How do you think your pattern of studying would differ between two courses, one of which has monthly exams and the other which has daily quizzes?

2. Would you work faster in a factory that paid you $10 for each television you assembled or one that paid you $10 for every five TVs you assembled?

3. Are you more likely to enjoy listening to a CD in which every song is good or a disc in which only two or three songs are good?

4. Why do you "channel surf" during commercials while watching a football game?

5. Would your pattern of casting differ if you reliably caught a fish after every 20 casts versus after a variable number of casts averaging about 20?

To answer all of these questions, you'd have to know something about schedules of reinforcement. In fact, it is hard to think of any behavior that is not affected by the consequence and the circumstances under which these consequences occur (i.e., schedules of reinforcement). Hence, an understanding of schedules is essential to understanding behavior.

Types of schedules of reinforcement

Every learning textbook provides definitions and descriptions of the following basic schedules of reinforcement: continuous reinforcement (CRF), fixed-ratio (FR), variable-ratio (VR), fixed-interval (FI), and variable-interval (VI). Some books provide definitions and descriptions of more schedules, such as fixed- and variable-time (FT and VT, respectively), fixed- and variable-duration (FD and VD, respectively), differential reinforcement of low rates (DRL), differential reinforcement of high rates (DRH), differential reinforcement of other behavior (DRO), and progressive ratio (PR). There are also variations of the basic schedules, such as a fixed- or variable-interval with a limited hold. Finally, any of these schedules can be combined to form tandem, multiple, and concurrent schedules, to name a few. In short, there are many ways to schedule consequences. Rather than restate what is written in your textbook, it is more important that we highlight those aspects of the basic schedules that distinguish them from each other and that affect behavior maintained on those schedules.

Distinguishing ratio schedules from interval schedules

One way to distinguish schedules of reinforcement is on the basis of [1] whether behavior alone is required for reinforcement, or [2] whether behavior and the passage of time are required. The former schedules are known as ratio schedules, and reinforcement is dependent only on some number of occurrences of the target response. The latter are known as interval schedules, and reinforcement depends on the occurrence of the target behavior *after a particular time*. This additional requirement -- that only behavior occurring after a particular time will be reinforced -- has a profound effect on behavior. For example, interval schedules generally support lower rates of responding than corresponding ratio schedules. Also, long fixed-interval schedules support increasingly faster (i.e., positively accelerating) responding followed by a pause after reinforcement, whereas fixed-ratio schedules tend to support a steady rate of responding followed by a pause after reinforcement.

Fixed schedules differ from variable schedules of reinforcement

Another way to distinguish schedules of reinforcement is on the basis of whether the schedule has constant or fixed behavioral and/or temporal requirements, or whether the schedule has changing or variable behavioral and/or temporal requirements. For example, in a FR 30 schedule, every 30th target response will be reinforced; however, in a VR 30 schedule, the number of responses required for reinforcement will, *on average*, be 30. On some occasions the value may be 1, on other occasions it might be 20, on others it might be 30, and still on others it might be 40 or 50. On average, though, 30 responses will be required for reinforcement. Whether a schedule has fixed or variable requirements from reinforcer to reinforcer has a significant effect on behavior. For example, fixed schedules tend to produce patterns of behavior that are interrupted by pauses after reinforcement; variable schedules produce steady responding with little or no pausing after reinforcement.

Feedback functions

One of the best means for understanding differences among schedules of reinforcement is to understand *feedback functions*, or the relations between response rate and reinforcement rate. To illustrate, consider a FR 5 schedule in which five responses produce one reinforcer. In this schedule, how often reinforcers occur depends exclusively on how rapidly the animal responds; reinforcement rate will always equal one-fifth of the response rate. In contrast, consider a FI 15-s schedule in which a response is reinforced if it occurs at least 15 seconds since the previous reinforcer. In this schedule, a response rate of 4 responses per minute matches the reinforcement rate. Slower response rates produce proportional changes in reinforcer rates, but faster response rates do not. That is, reinforcement rate ceases to vary with response rate. Differences in the feedback function explain why ratio schedules typically produce higher rates of responding than interval schedules.

Cumulative records

Perhaps the most common way of studying the effects of schedules of reinforcement is by examining cumulative records of responding across time. A cumulative record is a plot of the cumulative number of responses (on the *y*-axis) across time (on the *x*-axis). An example is shown in Fig 10.1.

Figure 10.1

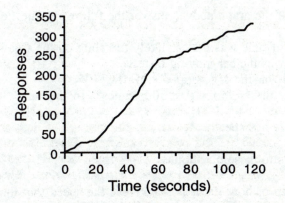

There are three important characteristics of cumulative records. First, because it is a *cumulative* record, each instance of a response is added to the previous number of responses. Responses can only accumulate or remain unchanged across time; they can never decrease over time. Second, the slope of a cumulative record is always positive or zero; it is never negative. Third, the slope provides information about the rate of behavior; a steep slope means fast responding and a shallow slope means slow responding.

An analogy that might help us further understand cumulative records is to consider an odometer on a car, which keeps a tally -- a cumulative record -- of the number of miles traveled. Like cumulative records, odometers never lose mileage; they only increase (when the car is moving) or remain unchanged (when the car in not in motion).

If you were to plot the number of miles traveled in a car across time, say, 60 minutes, you would obtain a graph in which the number of miles increased or remained unchanged during this time. The odometer would never lose miles. Now, think about the following two questions related to the second and third characteristics of cumulative records: What would make the odometer accumulate miles faster: driving 30 miles per hour (mph) or driving 60 mph? And, what speed would you be driving when the odometer was stationary (i.e., remaining unchanged): 0 mph, 30 mph, or 60 mph? Figure 10.2 shows how the number of miles on an odometer changed while a car was driven over the course of an hour through city streets and on a freeway.

Figure 10.2

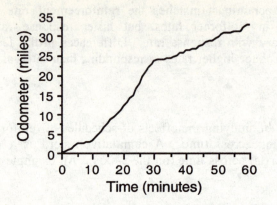

To check your understanding of the graph above, answer the following questions:

1.   During which period of time was the car likely traveling on the freeway?
2.   During which period was the car moving fastest?
3.   During which periods was the car stopped in traffic?
4.   How many miles were driven in the first 30 minutes? In the next 30 minutes? In the full 60 minutes?
5.   What was the car's average speed?

Now, let's examine the answers to these questions.

1.   The slope -- how steep or how flat it is -- conveys the speed that the car was traveling; more miles will accumulate on the odometer when the car was travelling swiftly, and thus the slope is relatively steep. In general, the slope between the 10- and 30-minute mark is relatively steep, suggesting that this was the time that the car was on the freeway.

2.   Within these 20 minutes, the slope is steepest between the 25- and 30-minute mark, meaning that the car was traveling fastest during this period.

3.   A flat slope means that the odometer is not changing. An unchanging odometer means that the car is not moving; therefore, these are the periods that the car was stopped in traffic. These occurred most noticeably between the 5- and 10-minute mark, the 30- and 35-minute mark, and the 50- and 55-minute mark.

4.   Although approximate values can be read from the graph, the odometer read 000028.3 after 30 minutes and 000033.0 after 60 minutes. Thus, 28.3 miles were driven during the first 30 minutes, 4.7 miles were driven during the next 30 minutes, and 33 miles were driven during the full 60 minutes.

5.   The car traveled 33 miles in 1 hour (60 minutes); thus, the average speed was 33 mph.

Reading and understanding cumulative records is no different from reading and understanding the graph in Fig 10.2. The only major difference is that the *y*-axis consists of the cumulative number of responses instead of miles; the *x*-axis in both cases is time. To bring this message home, look again at Figs 10.1 and 10.2. Do you notice anything similar about them? To check your understanding, answer the following questions about Fig 10.1:

1.   During which period of time was the animal responding rapidly?
2.   During which period was the animal responding fastest?
3.   During which periods were the animal not responding?
4.   How many responses occurred in each block of 30 minutes?
5.   What was the animal's average rate of responding?

EXERCISES

10-1: Describe each of the following schedules of reinforcement: (a) continuous reinforcement, (b) fixed-ratio, (c) variable-ratio, (d) fixed-interval, and (e) variable-interval.

10-2: In the space below each graph, write the name of the schedule of reinforcement that most likely produced the adjacent cumulative record. (Note that Graphs C and D are not identical.)

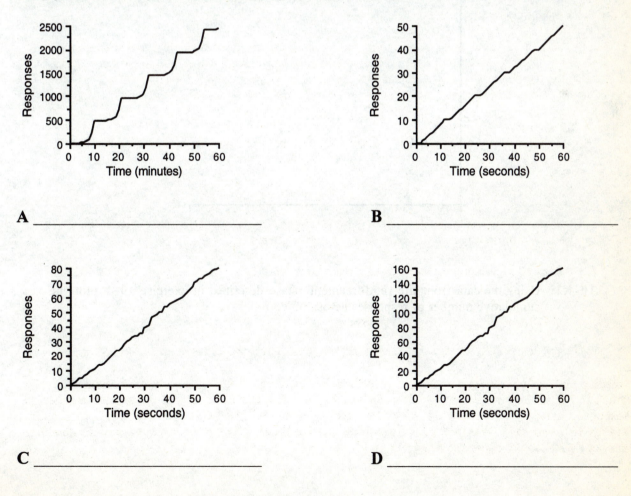

A _____

B _____

C _____

D _____

10-3: Explain what is wrong with the following "cumulative record":

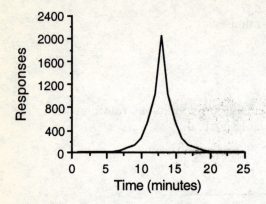

10-4: An experiment in which a child pressed a button to earn candy yielded the following number of responses in successive 10-s periods: 0, 1, 2, 1, 3, 4, 6, 9, 10, 7, 9, 8, 9. Then, during extinction, the following results were obtained in successive 10-s periods: 9, 7, 6, 4, 2, 3, 2, 1, 2, 1, 1, 0, 0, 0, 0, 0.

10-4.1: Plot the *response rate* across time. Separate the reinforcement and extinction phases with a vertical line, and do not connect the points across the two phases.

10-4.2: Using the data from the reinforcement phase described in exercise **10-4**, plot the cumulative number of responses across time.

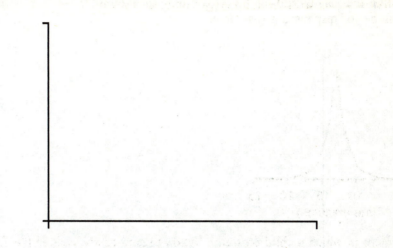

10-4.3: Using the data from the extinction phase described in exercise **10-4**, plot the cumulative number of responses across time.

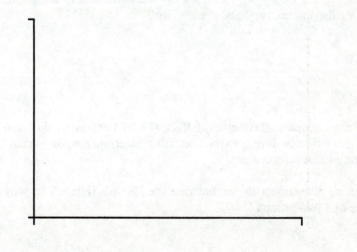

10-4.4: What was the average response rate during the reinforcement phase? What was the average response rate during the extinction phase?

10-5: As in the experiment above, a child's buttonpresses were reinforced, and yielded the following number of responses across successive 10-s periods: 0, 2, 4, 2, 6, 8, 12, 19, 20, 14, 18, 16, 18.

10-5.1: Using the same scale for the *y*-axis used in exercise **10-4.2**, plot the cumulative number of responses across time.

10-5.2: Comparing the data from exercises **10-4.2** and **10-5.1**, what information does the slope of the line convey about behavior?

10-6: The Partial Reinforcement Extinction Effect (PREE) refers to the observation that behavior generally decreases more slowly during extinction after intermittent or partial reinforcement than it does following continuous reinforcement.

10-6.1: Design an experiment to demonstrate the PREE. [Hint: You will need at least two phases and two groups.]

10-6.2: In the graph on the next page, draw hypothetical results of your experiment. Separate the phases of your experiment with vertical lines, and be sure to label clearly all aspects of your graph.

10-6.3: Let's reexamine the dependent measure you chose for your hypothetical experiment. Because the rate of responding during partial reinforcement is often greater than the rate of responding during continuous reinforcement, some researchers have suggested that simply comparing changes in response rates across extinction is not an appropriate measure for detecting the PREE. In other words, because response rates between the continuous and partial reinforcement groups are already different during the reinforcement phase, we should not be surprised that the group with the higher response rate (typically, the partial reinforcement group) continues to respond more during extinction than the group with the lower response rate (typically, the continuous reinforcement group). Given this information, come up with a better dependent measure for assessing whether the PREE occurred. [Hint: Think about *proportions* of responding.]

10-6.4: In the graph below, redraw the curves from exercise **10-6.2** using your new dependent measure.

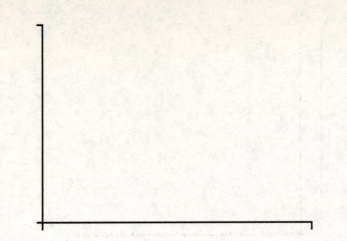

10-7: As summarized above, a function that shows how average response rate relates to average reinforcement rate is called a *feedback function*. Draw feedback functions for the following schedules: FR-40, VR-80, and VI-120-s.

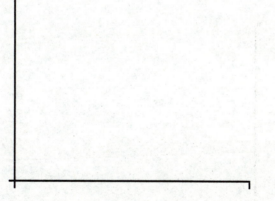

10-8: Suppose that a psychologist has set up an experiment using two birds, Pigeon A and Pigeon B. The birds are placed in separate operant conditioning chambers and cannot see, hear, or otherwise sense each other. Pigeon A's pecking is reinforced on a VR 20 schedule. Pigeon B's pecking is reinforced whenever Pigeon A earns a reinforcer.

10-8.1: What is Pigeon B's schedule of reinforcement? Explain.

10-8.2: Which bird will peck at a higher rate? Explain.

10-8.3: Now let's assume that no target response, such as pecking, was required of Pigeon B. What kind of behavior would you expect this bird to engage in? [Hint: Look for *superstition*, *superstitious behavior*, and/or *fixed-time (FT)* schedules of reinforcement in the index of your primary textbook.]

10-9: It has been said that schedules of reinforcement can explain much of human behavior. In a short essay, describe how schedules of reinforcement can explain each of the following distinctions: "energetic" vs. "lazy" people, "motivated" vs. "unmotivated" individuals, and "persistent" people vs. "quitters."

11

PUNISHMENT, ESCAPE, AND AVOIDANCE

Major topics covered in the exercises of this chapter:

Avoidance conditioning, escape conditioning, negative reinforcement, punishment, two-process theory

Two-process theory and negative reinforcement

Although operant and Pavlovian conditioning seem clearly distinguishable, "elements" of each are often present in the procedures of the other. In this sense, it is perhaps better to conceive of operant and Pavlovian conditioning as analogous to elemental hydrogen and oxygen. These two elements are rare in nature, but their combination in the form of water is common. Similarly, most learned behavior is a mixture in varying proportions of operant and Pavlovian conditioning.

Two-process theory (sometimes also called *two-factor theory*) describes the interaction between operant and Pavlovian elements, and common examples are found in situations where animals have to avoid aversive outcomes. For example, a gopher that sees a hawk overhead will not wait to see what the bird will do; upon sensing the hawk, the gopher will retreat to its burrow. In the laboratory, a dog will jump over a hurdle during a tone if this response prevents the delivery of shock. In these and similar circumstances, the sight of the hawk or the sound of the tone predicts an aversive outcome (e.g., being attacked or shocked) unless a certain response occurs (e.g., retreating to a burrow or jumping a hurdle). The relation between the signal and the aversive event is a Pavlovian CS-US relation; but, because responding during the CS allows the animal to avoid the aversive event, this response is negatively reinforced (an operant, response-consequence relation). An event or object is a *negative reinforcer* if it increases the likelihood of a behavior that removes or terminates the event or object.

Punishment

Anything that is a negative reinforcer can also function as a *punisher* when it follows a response. A punisher weakens or decreases the strength of the behavior that produces it. Thus, all negative reinforcers are punishers, and vice versa; one focuses on the ability of a stimulus to increase behavior that terminates or "shuts off" the stimulus (negative reinforcement); the other focuses on the ability of this same stimulus to decrease behavior which causes or "turns on" the stimulus (punishment).

EXERCISES

11-1: Define the following terms: *punisher, negative reinforcer, escape conditioning, avoidance conditioning.*

11-2: With respect to whether a stimulus is presented or removed and the effect of that presentation or removal on subsequent behavior, distinguish among a positive reinforcer, a punisher, and a negative reinforcer by circling the appropriate stimulus within each major cell in the table below.

	Behavior causes the **presentation** of a stimulus	Behavior causes the **removal** of a stimulus
The contingency causes an **increase** in behavior	positive reinforcer negative reinforcer punisher	positive reinforcer negative reinforcer punisher
The contingency causes a **decrease** in behavior	positive reinforcer negative reinforcer punisher	positive reinforcer negative reinforcer punisher

11-3: Punishers are most effective when they are presented immediately after a response. Consider a situation involving a straight-alley runway with a start box at one end and a goal box at the other end. After having been trained to run down the alley for a piece of food, different groups of rats began receiving a mild electric shock 0, 1, 2, 4, 8, or 16 seconds after they reached the goal box. Draw a graph showing how running speed (the *y*-axis) changed as a function of the number of trials (*x*-axis). You will need 6 curves, one for each delay.

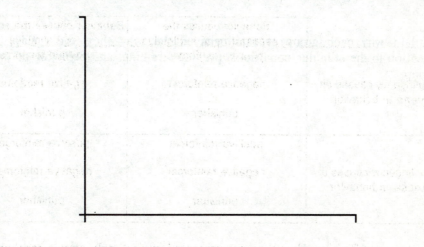

11-4: Punishers presented after every instance of a response are more effective than punishers presented intermittently. Draw and explain a graph that depicts the functional relation between the effectiveness of a punisher and its schedule of presentation.

11-5: Although punishment can be used to suppress many responses, it sometimes does not work well for eliminating escape responses. To illustrate, consider a situation in which three groups of rats were placed in a straight-alley runway in which the start box and the alley, but not the goal box, were electrified. All animals learned to quickly run down the alley to escape the shock. Once this escape response was well established, a new phase of the experiment began. For one group, no part of the runway was electrified. For a second group, only the alley was electrified; i.e., neither the start nor the goal box was electrified. For the third group, only the goal box was electrified.

Interestingly, the results showed that the first group's running speed decreased steadily across days. However, both the second and the third groups' running speeds remained relatively constant and high across days.

11-5.1: In the graph below, plot how running speed changed across days for all three groups of rats.

11-5.2: Explain why each group of rats behaved the way they did. Pay particular attention to the stimulus conditions, previous training, and behavior of the second group.

11-6: Punishers are less effective when the motivation to engage in the unwanted behavior is high. Draw and explain a graph that depicts a functional relation between the effectiveness of a punisher and an animal's motivation to respond. Be sure to come up with a plausible operational definition for "motivation" (i.e., it should be quantifiable).

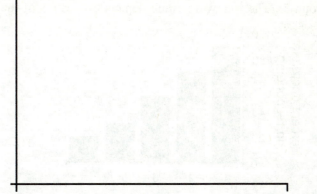

11-7: Punishers are more effective when there is another way for animals to earn reinforcers that are being lost because a response is being punished. Draw and explain a graph that depicts a functional relation between the effectiveness of a punisher and the availability of alternative behavior to earn reinforcers.

11-8: Consider the following situation involving five groups of hungry rats that were leverpressing for food. After each animal earned 500 reinforcers, a new phase of the experiment began.

In Phase 2, each leverpress now produced a shock rather than food. Different groups of rats received different intensities of shock. For Group 1, each leverpress produced a 10-mA shock. For Group 2, the first leverpress produced a 2-mA shock, and then the next four leverpresses each produced a 10-mA shock. For Group 3, the first five leverpresses produced shocks of 2, 4, 10, 10, and 10 mA, respectively. For Group 4, the sequence of shocks was 2, 4, 6, 10, and 10 mA; for Group 5 the sequence of shocks was 2, 4, 6, 8, and 10 mA.

After five leverpresses, the experimenter noticed that leverpressing was suppressed most in Group 1 and least in Group 5. The following graph depicts the results of the experiment.

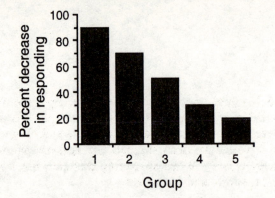

11-8.1: What can we conclude about the relationship between the effectiveness of a punisher and the manner (i.e., whether the intensity is introduced gradually or abruptly) in which it is introduced?

11-8.2: Given the experiment summarized above, briefly describe a possible confounding variable that might explain the results. Design an experiment to control for this confounding variable.

11-9: A characteristic of some avoidance behavior is that it is very resistant to extinction. Thus, in some circumstances, a person or animal may keep emitting avoidance behavior long after the aversive stimulus is removed from the situation. For example, a dog trained to jump over a barrier during a warning signal (e.g., a tone) that predicted occurrences of an aversive event (e.g., shock) may continue to do so even if the signal is never again followed by the aversive event. Using what you know about Pavlovian and operant contingencies, explain why avoidance behavior can be resistant to extinction.

11-10: A casual observation of behavioral control techniques used by governments, employers, and educators (among others) will reveal a propensity for aversive control. For example, it is unlikely that any driver has been pulled over by a police officer and given a $50 reward for driving at the correct speed; however, countless drivers have been stopped and issued citations for driving too fast. Why do you suppose this asymmetry exists? When answering this question, consider how reinforcers vs. punishers impact behavior in the short- and long-term.

11-11: Some scientists have suggested that punishment is ineffective for long-term suppression of unwanted behavior. To see why, consider an omission training procedure (also known as *negative punishment*, *time-out*, and *response cost*) in which an illuminated key (CS) is followed by the delivery of food (US) if a pigeon does not peck the key; pecking the key causes the omission of food. Under normal circumstances, briefly illuminating a key and following it by food causes pigeons to peck the key, a phenomena known as *autoshaping*. Many studies have shown that pigeons peck the key less when pecks cause the omission of food than when they do not (i.e., during autoshaping). The following sequence of 15 trials illustrates what happens during omission training:

TRIAL #	CS STATUS	RESPONSE	US STATUS
101	CS Presented	No Pecking	US Presented
102	CS Presented	No Pecking	US Presented
103	CS Presented	No Pecking	US Presented
104	CS Presented	Pecking	US Omitted
105	CS Presented	Pecking	US Omitted
106	CS Presented	No Pecking	US Presented
107	CS Presented	No Pecking	US Presented
108	CS Presented	Pecking	US Omitted
109	CS Presented	Pecking	US Omitted
110	CS Presented	Pecking	US Omitted
111	CS Presented	No Pecking	US Presented
112	CS Presented	No Pecking	US Presented
113	CS Presented	No Pecking	US Presented
114	CS Presented	No Pecking	US Presented
115	CS Presented	Pecking	US Omitted

11-11.1: Given the sequence above, explain why pecking continues to occur even after numerous omissions of the food. [Hint: Consider the interaction between Pavlovian and operant contingencies.]

11-11.2: Describe a general reason for why punishment might not suppress unwanted behavior in the long run? Again, to answer this question, think about how behavior is controlled by operant and Pavlovian contingencies.

11-12: According to the two-process theory of avoidance, a response during the CS is negatively reinforced by "fear reduction." To assess whether fear is reduced following an avoidance response, researchers have measured physiological assays of fear (e.g., heart rate, respiration). These studies have yielded inconclusive results: Sometimes there is a difference in the physiological correlates of fear before and after an avoidance response; sometimes there is no difference. These results have led some learning theorists to conclude that avoidance behavior is not reinforced by a reduction in fear. More generally, these theorists assert that there is no stimulus change at all following an avoidance response (i.e., the stimulus conditions before and after an avoidance response are identical). Given that studies have failed to reliably demonstrate the occurrence of fear reduction or any stimulus change before and after an avoidance response, some researchers have concluded that two-process theory of avoidance cannot be correct because there is no immediate reinforcer for the avoidance response.

Evaluate the argument that there is no stimulus change following an avoidance response. Which stimuli, if any, might differ before and after an avoidance response?

11-13: A critical assumption of two-process theory is that there are two distinct types of contingencies (Pavlovian and operant) and one cannot be reduced to the other. Later, you will be asked to design an experiment to evaluate this assumption. However, for the moment, let's attack this problem in several steps.

11-13.1: Let's begin by considering the example of Pavlovian conditioning of a human eye-blink in which a tone is the CS and a puff of air to the eye is the US. Eventually, the person will blink (the CR) when the tone (the CS) is presented. Explain how the development of blinking during the CS might be the result of operant and not Pavlovian conditioning. [Hint: Might the blink during the CS serve some purpose? If so, what is it?]

11-13.2: Does blinking during the CS allow the person to avoid a stimulus? If so, which one?

11-13.3: If you have answered the previous questions correctly, then you have identified how operant, and not Pavlovian conditioning, could produce blinking during the CS. You should also have identified how blinking during the CS reduces the intensity of or eliminates a particular stimulus. In general, what effect does eliminating or reducing the intensity of the US have on the CR? [Hint: See Chapters 4, 5, and 6.]

11-13.4: Now, imagine a situation in which omitting the US contingent upon a CR causes the CR to occur *more* often or intensely. In general, this effect is inconsistent with CRs resulting from Pavlovian conditioning. (Again, return to Chapters 4, 5, and 6 if this is unfamiliar.) How should this effect be interpreted?

11-13.5: Using the information in exercises **11-13.1** through **11-13.4**, design an experiment to test whether there are two distinct types of contingencies (Pavlovian and operant) and one cannot be reduced to the other. [Hint: The key comparison will be between a group of subjects (let's call them Group Omission) in which the US is omitted contingent upon a CR and a group of subjects (let's call them Group Yoked) in which their US is omitted whenever a yoked subject in Group Omission emits a CR.] Be sure to specify the independent variable(s), dependent variable(s), and how various outcomes support or refute the major assumption of two-process theory (i.e., that there are two distinct types of contingencies).

12

"SIMPLE" STIMULUS CONTROL

Major topics covered in the exercises of this chapter:

Stimulus discrimination, stimulus generalization, excitatory generalization gradients, inhibitory generalization gradients, peak shift, transposition, stimulus control

Stimulus control

No action occurs in a vacuum. All behavior occurs in a context; all responses occur in the presence of stimuli. The list of examples is endless: You say "hello" (response) after picking up a ringing telephone (stimulus), you step on the accelerator (response) when the traffic light turns green (stimulus), you depress the brake pedal (response) when the traffic light is red (stimulus), you lower your voice (response) when you enter a church (stimulus), you raise your voice (response) when you enter a nightclub (stimulus), you throw a ball (response) at someone who's wearing a baseball glove (stimulus), you approach the pick-up window (response) after the clerk calls out your number (stimulus), and you open an umbrella (response) when it begins to rain (stimulus). If in the presence of particular stimuli you emit one response but in the presence of other stimuli you emit other responses, then those stimuli are controlling your behavior. How stimuli come to control behavior is a matter of stimulus discrimination training.

Pavlovian stimulus discrimination

During Pavlovian conditioning, stimulus discrimination training consists of presenting a US following one CS (the CS+) but not following another CS (the CS-). For example, if a light is followed by the presentation of food but a ringing bell is not, then a hungry dog will eventually salivate during the light but not the bell. A simpler form of discrimination takes place when behavior occurs only in the presence of one stimulus (or stimulus set, sometimes called a "context"), but not at other times. Thus, if the dog in the preceding example is trained only with red light-food pairings, then it may salivate much less when it is presented with a green light during a test trial -- even though it was salivating reliably and vigorously during the red light.

Fig 12.1 shows two ways that Pavlovian stimulus discrimination is commonly depicted in graphs. The left panel shows how the CR changed across trials during conditioning; the right panel shows the intensity of CRs elicited during presentations of different stimuli -- in this case, pictures of circles of different diameters -- during a test session following conditioning. The CS was a 5-cm diameter circle presented for 8 sec before the presentation of grain (the US). Test sessions of this kind are normally done during extinction (i.e., without any US presentations).

Figure 12.1

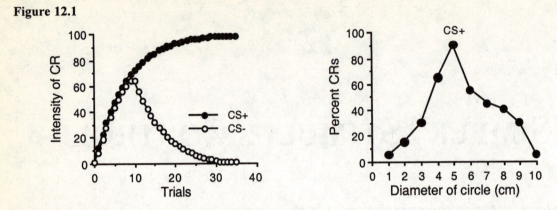

Operant stimulus discrimination

During operant conditioning, stimulus discrimination training consists of differentially reinforcing a target response in the presence of different stimuli. For example, if a pigeon is reinforced for pecking a yellow light but not an orange light, the pigeon will eventually restrict its pecks to the yellow light. Similarly, a pigeon that is reinforced for pecking a green light on a VI 10-sec schedule and a red light on a VI 120-sec schedule will spend more time pecking the green light. An even simpler form of discrimination takes place when behavior occurs only in the presence of one stimulus (or a set of stimuli) but not elsewhere. For example, a pigeon reinforced for pecking any colored light might not do so if the fan that normally ventilates the experimental chamber is not turned on.

Graphically, stimulus control arising from operant stimulus discrimination training is depicted in the same manner used to show control by various dimensions of CSs. Fig 12.2 shows two examples. See if you can provide a description of the graphs.

Figure 12.2

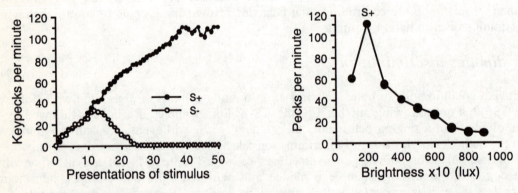

Stimulus generalization

When we speak of *discrimination*, we are emphasizing the fact that behavior does not occur equally in the presence of all stimuli. However, when we speak of *generalization*, we are emphasizing that control by one stimulus extends to some other stimuli. In this regard, stimulus discrimination and generalization are properties of the same coin (so to speak)

In Pavlovian conditioning, generalization refers to the fact that stimuli other than the CS+ elicit a CR (or inhibit the CR, in the case of a CS-), though the intensity or frequency of the CR may be diminished. The important point is that stimuli similar to the CS+ and the CS- do elicit or inhibit a CR, respectively. Similarly, in operant conditioning, generalization refers to the fact stimuli similar to S+ control the target response, and that stimuli similar to the S- suppress or inhibit the target response.

Peak shift

Following some instances of stimulus discrimination training involving an explicit S+ and S-, animals sometimes show a curious effect during generalization tests: The stimulus that supports the most responding is not the S+, but a stimulus on the "side" of the S+ that is even farther from the S-. This phenomenon is known as *peak shift*. An example is presented in Fig 12.3. One reason that peak shift is an important phenomenon is because it is an instance when a stimulus that was not used in training controls more responding than a stimulus explicitly associated with reinforcement. To understand why peak shift occurs, we need to consider excitatory generalization gradients that develop around the S+ and inhibitory generalization gradients that develop around the S-.

Figure 12.3

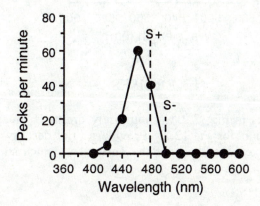

Excitatory and inhibitory generalization gradients

As we noted above, the degree that stimuli other than the S+ control responding is a matter of stimulus generalization. However, it is also possible to determine the degree that stimuli other than the S- control nonresponding. The generalization gradient that develops around an S+ is said to be an *excitatory generalization gradient*; the gradient that develops around an S- is said to be an *inhibitory generalization gradient*. An example of these gradients is illustrated in Fig 12.4.

Figure 12.4

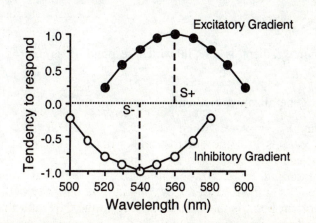

It should be evident from the graph that when an S+ and an S- are similar enough along some dimension (e.g., color), the summation of the excitatory and inhibitory gradients around each stimulus will result in a net excitatory gradient whose peak has shifted to the side of the S+ away from the S-. The result of this summation -- the peak shift -- is illustrated in Fig 12.5.

Figure 12.5

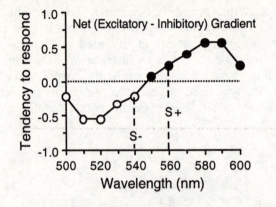

EXERCISES

12-1: A description of the graphs in Fig 12.2 was purposely omitted. Imagine now that you have been asked to write a figure caption for Fig 12.2. Provide a brief description of each graph, being sure to say something about the axes, the shape of the curve, and which stimuli controlled the most and least responding.

12-2: A flat generalization gradient is one in which responding is approximately equal across all values of a stimulus.

   12-2.1: Draw a flat generalization gradient.

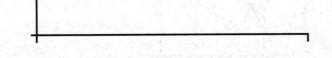

12-2.2: Provide 2 reasons for why flat generalization gradients might occur.

12-3: On the graph below, draw 3 curves that illustrate different amounts of stimulus generalization. The dependent variable for the *y*-axis should be *pecks per minute* and the independent variables for the *x*-axis are different *colors of light*. For simplicity, label the horizontal axis with 7 colors of light: red, orange, yellow, green, blue, indigo, and violet (in that order). Assume that the S+ was red.

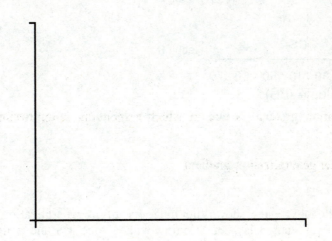

12-4: Examine the graph below that contains the results of a test session in which a pigeon was presented with different colored pecking keys. Describe a plausible (and relatively simple) situation that would produce the outcome depicted in the graph. [Hint: Consider the possibility that there are more than one S+ and more than one S-, and that there were different schedules of reinforcement correlated with the different stimuli during training.]

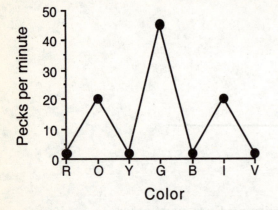

12-5: The graph below shows the generalization gradient for 3 rabbits presented with a brief tone (CS+) before water was squirted into their mouths (US). Each rabbit's data are depicted by a curve: solid black circles for Rabbit 1, open white circles for Rabbit 2, and solid black triangles for Rabbit 3. Briefly describe which rabbit showed the most stimulus generalization, being sure to state clearly your operational definition of *most stimulus generalization*.

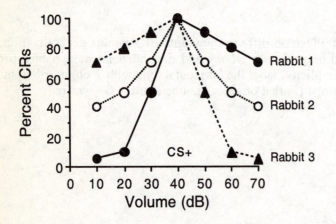

12-6: The graph on the next page shows the outcome of a generalization test following many sessions of "standard" Pavlovian delay conditioning with a tone CS and a mild electric shock US. The subject in the experiment was a male college student with normal hearing.

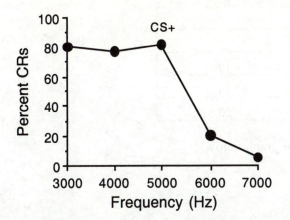

12-6.1: Briefly describe the graph.

12-6.2: What is unusual about the results? Be sure to refer to stimulus discrimination and generalization in your answer.

12-6.3: Speculate as to why these results might have been obtained.

12-7: A dog is presented with a picture of a 10-cm diameter circle (CS), and then food (US) is placed in its mouth. Once the dog is reliably salivating during presentations of the CS, the experiment enters a new phase. The new phase consists of a single session in which the dog is given 20 randomized presentations of each of the following stimuli during extinction: a 30-cm diameter circle, a 20-cm circle, a 10-cm circle, a 5-cm circle, and a 1-cm circle. The table below shows the number of presentations in which there was an increase in salivation above the amount that occurred during the preceding intertrial interval. (This was the operational definition of a CR used in the experiment.)

Diameter of Circle (cm)	Stimuli with a CR
1	1
5	2
10	19
20	18
30	20

12-7.1: Plot the data from the test session in the graph below.

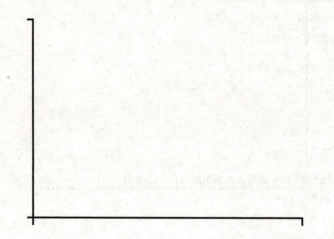

12-7.2: Speculate as to what might have caused these results. Compare your answer to the one you provided for exercise **12-6.3**.

12-7.3: Describe an experiment to test the idea you described in exercise **12-7.2**.

12-8: A pigeon learned to peck a key that showed a horizontal (0 degrees) white line on a dark background. After 10 days of training with a VI 60-sec schedule, a test session began. During the test session, reinforcement was never presented, and the line on the key was tilted from -90 to +90 degrees in steps of 30 degrees. For example, for the first 30 sec, the key might have displayed a line tilted -30 degrees, for the next 30 sec it displayed a line tilted +60 degrees, and so on.

12-8.1: In the space below, draw a plausible graph showing how response rate likely changed in the presence of each line tilt. (Note that -90 degrees is the same as +90 degrees.)

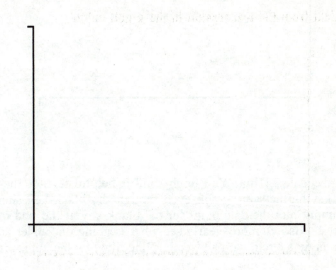

12-8.2: What does this experiment illustrate?

12-9: In one study, pigeons were presented with either a blank (white) key or with a white key on which was superimposed a black line at 90 degrees (vertical). In the presence of the blank key, responses were reinforced according to a VI schedule. In the presence of the 90-degree line, responses were not reinforced. Then, during a generalization test, the results shown in the table below were obtained.

Line Tilt (degrees)	Number of Responses
0	195
+30	175
+60	110
+90	85
+120	115
+150	185
+180	200
blank	520

12-9.1: Plot the data in a graph, being sure to label the S+ and S-.

12-9.2: Interpret the data. [Hint: You might find it helpful to plot the responses during the blank key on the same graph even though the blank key showed no line. To do this, simply plot the data point for the blank key at the end of the *x*-axis after 180 degrees. Also, to more clearly see what is going on, under each tick mark on the *x*-axis, draw a circle with a bisecting line tilted by the appropriate angle.]

12-9.3: What type of control (excitatory and/or inhibitory) does the generalization gradient show? Explain your answer.

12-10: Consider the following experiment. A chimpanzee was presented repeatedly with two cards: one 9 cm x 12 cm, the other 12 cm x 16 cm. When the chimp pointed to the latter card, it received food; when the chimp pointed to the former card, it did not receive food. Once the discrimination was well established, the chimp was given a test trial in which the 12-cm x 16-cm card was paired with a new card whose dimensions were 15 cm x 20 cm. Food was not presented during the test trials.

The results showed that the chimp preferred the larger card on more than 90% of the test trials. This outcome seems surprising because the chimp preferred the card that was never associated with food (the 15-cm x 20-cm card) rather than the card that was always associated with food (the 12-cm x 16-cm card).

With reference to peak shift, explain the results of the experiment. Show your reasoning in a graph.

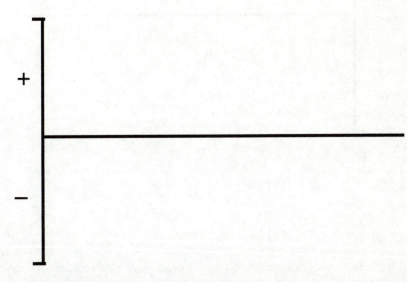

12-11: Further experiments showed that chimps will prefer the 12-cm x 16-cm card (the card associated with food) if the new card presented during the test is much larger (e.g., 21 cm x 28 cm) than the training card. Why? Provide a graph to illustrate your answer.

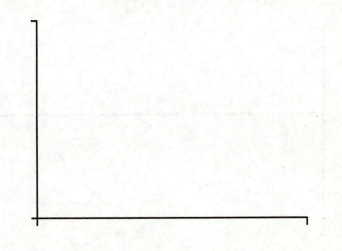

12-12: With reference to excitatory and inhibitory gradients (and their relation to peak shift), describe how you would do the following:

12-12.1: Sharpen a generalization gradient. Be sure to include a graph with your answer, and to label and describe your graph.

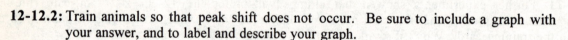

12-12.2: Train animals so that peak shift does not occur. Be sure to include a graph with your answer, and to label and describe your graph.

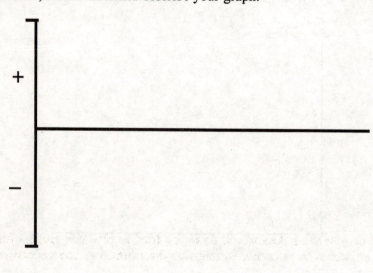

12-13: Consider the following situation. A father holds a small orange ball in his hands. His 2-year old daughter, Ana, stretches her arms toward the ball, a behavior that in the past got her the ball. This time the father does not give her the ball. Instead, he says <u>loudly</u>, "Ana, say *Give*." Having learned to imitate simple words before, Ana repeats *Give* and immediately receives the ball. A few seconds later, the father holds the ball and again refuses to give it to Ana when she simply stretches her arms. He says in a <u>low</u> voice *Give*, and when Ana repeats the word, he gives her the ball. On a third trial, while holding the ball, the father <u>whispers</u> *Give*. Ana receives the ball when she says *Give*. On a fourth trial, the father <u>simply moves his lips </u>as if saying *Give*, but no sound is produced. Again, Ana gets the ball when she says *Give*. Finally, the father <u>holds the ball</u> without providing any verbal prompts. After a few seconds, Ana says *Give*, and the father responds to her request. The following day, when the father played with Ana, she was given the ball only after she said *Give*.

> **12-13.1:** Describe all the principles of learning in the above interaction. Be careful to identify and explain clearly each element of the principle (e.g., response, consequences, contingencies of reinforcement, S+, S-, etc).

> **12-13.2:** What do you think Ana would do if you tried to play this game with her? Explain your answer with reference to stimulus discrimination and generalization.

13

"COMPLEX" STIMULUS CONTROL

Major topics covered in the exercises of this chapter:

Memory, remembering, concepts, concept formation, temporal discrimination ("timing"), numerical discrimination, serial position effect

"Complex" stimulus control

Whereas the previous chapter dealt with relatively simple stimulus control -- meaning that the stimuli controlling behavior were always present when the behavior occurred and varied only along one or two dimensions -- this chapter deals with more complex forms of stimulus control. The first of these involves situations in which a stimulus is not present when the behavior it controls occurs. These types of situations are used to study *memory* or *remembering*. A second type of complex stimulus control occurs when multiple stimuli, perhaps sharing common elements, control behavior. These types of situations involve *concepts* or *concept formation*. The third and last type of complex stimulus control we will consider involves situations in which the temporal and numerical attributes of stimuli control behavior. These situations are often said to involve *temporal* and *numerosity* discrimination.

Memory

Consider a rabbit that, after many pairings of a light and a puff of air to its eye, blinks when it sees the light that normally precedes the airpuff. This is a relatively simple form of Pavlovian conditioning that leads to learning about the light-airpuff relationship. However, for learning to occur, physiological changes must take place that permit the "recording" of the light-airpuff association in such a way that each presentation of the light and airpuff is not a novel presentation. These recordings are referred to in everyday language as *memory* or *remembering*. Within the study of learning, memory is most often studied using variations of two major procedures: *delayed matching-to-sample* and *the radial-arm maze*.

    Delayed Matching-to-Sample (DMTS). A common form of the DMTS procedure involves presenting an animal with a stimulus that it needs to remember, such as a red key presented in the center of three keys in a horizontal row. This to-be-remembered key is called the *sample stimulus*. After the animal makes a response which indicates that it has seen the sample stimulus (e.g., pecking or pressing it), the sample is removed and a delay period begins. Following the delay, *comparison stimuli* are presented, such as a red and a green key, and the animal is required to choose the stimulus that matches the sample (in our example, the red key). If it makes the correct response, the animal is rewarded; if it makes an incorrect response, the stimuli are removed and no reward is presented. Thus, as the name implies, the objective is to select, after a delay, the comparison stimulus that matches the sample stimulus. Fig 13.1 shows a schematic of the DMTS procedure described above.

With this procedure, there are many ways that one can study an animal's memory. For example, the duration of the delay could be varied. Can you think of other ways that the DMTS procedure can be modified to study memory?

Figure 13.1

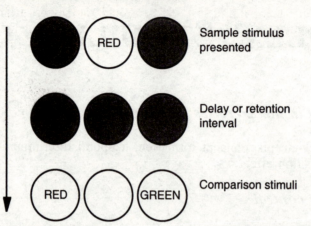

Delayed Matching-to-Sample

Sample stimulus presented

Delay or retention interval

Comparison stimuli

Radial-Arm Maze. A radial-arm maze usually contains eight arms or alleys, each of which originates in a central hub and ends with a food cup. From the hub, the animal -- typically a rat -- can choose to traverse any of the arms. After entering an arm and consuming the food, the animal must return to the hub before it can enter any other arm. Fig 13.2 shows a stylized drawing of an eight-arm radial maze.

Figure 13.2

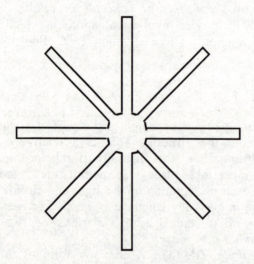

With this simple apparatus, experimenters can study animal memory by, for example, seeing how many errors a rat makes by revisiting an arm from which it has already eaten the food. Similarly, a rat could be allowed to eat the food from four arms and then be taken to its home cage for a period of time. Following this "rest" period, the rat could be returned to the maze to see if it can remember which arms it depleted of food. Can you think of other ways that the radial-arm maze can be used to study memory?

Concepts

Stimuli that cannot readily be reduced to a set of distinguishing elements are called *concepts* or *categories*. Humans, trees, fish, love, and evil are all examples of concepts. Although the elements that distinguish colors or shapes are more easily identified than those that distinguish, say, instances of love, the ability to identify red, green, triangle, and rectangle also requires concept formation. For example, which of the following stimuli in Fig 13.3 would you say are triangles? Which would a 3-year-old child identify as triangles? Which would a 12-year-old child say are triangles? Which would a mathematician identify as triangles? That different people identify different stimuli as triangles means that their concept of triangle differs.

Figure 13.3

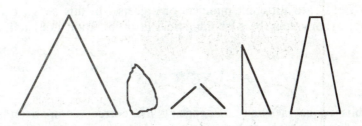

But how do people and animals learn concepts? The general answer is that they learn them the same way they learn any discrimination -- by being reinforced for correct responses in the presence of particular stimuli and not reinforced for incorrect responses in the presence of other stimuli. For example, to teach pigeons the concept *tree*, Richard Herrnstein and his collaborators showed them slides containing a single tree, several trees, or pieces of trees (such as a branch). Pecking a response key when a slide showed a tree resulted in food reinforcement on a VI schedule. If a slide did not contain a tree, pecking at the response key was not reinforced. With this training procedure, pigeons learned to discriminate between slides containing trees from those that did not -- even though there were no common elements to the slides of trees or to the slides of nontrees. Some slides of trees consisted of pictures of green leaves; some slides of nontrees consisted of pictures of green grassy areas; some slides of trees consisted of leaves in their fall colors; some slides of nontrees consisted of celery stalks with their leafy tops.

So, how did the pigeons learn the concept *tree*? As with almost all phenomena under the heading "complex stimulus control," the answer is a matter of controversy. However, it appears that the pigeons in this case (and people and other animals in other cases) might have learned something about the relationship among the features in the slides of trees versus nontrees.

Temporal discrimination ("timing")

Temporal variables play a fundamental role in all aspects of learning -- habituation, Pavlovian, and operant conditioning. But time may also be more directly involved in learning, as when animals learn to act according to the temporal attributes of a stimulus. For example, rats, pigeons, monkeys, and other vertebrates can learn to behave in one manner after a 2-sec stimulus and in another manner after an 8-sec stimulus. And when a reinforcer such as food is available periodically, such as during an FI schedule, animals learn to pause immediately after food and then, about midway through the interval, begin responding at an increasingly faster rate until reinforcement.

A major empirical finding that has emerged from studies of timing is the *scalar property* of temporal discrimination. Metaphorically speaking, this property states that all temporal judgments are relative. Hence, how a rat behaves at 10 sec when reinforcement occurs every 30 sec is similar to how it behaves at 20 sec when reinforcement occurs every 60 sec. Similarly, having learned to press a left lever after a 2-sec signal and a right lever after an 8-sec signal, a rat will be indifferent (i.e., it is just as likely to press the left as the right lever) between the two levers when presented with a 4-sec signal, because 2 is to 4 as 4 is to 8. The scalar property gets its name from the fact that, when the intervals of a temporal discrimination change, the animal's performance is scaled (stretched or shrunk) by the same factor. Why the scalar property occurs is a matter of controversy.

Numerical discrimination

When an animal responds to a number, such as the number of objects displayed on a screen, it is engaging in numerical behavior. Thus, numerical discrimination occurs when animals can distinguish between different numbers of objects. In everyday language, this type of behavior is sometimes referred to as *counting*. However, technically, and at the very least, counting involves attaching a unique label (i.e., numerals, such as 1, 2, 3, etc.) from a fixed sequence of labels (e.g., 1, 2, 3, etc., rather than 1, 4, 2, 7, 3, …) to different numbers of objects. In this sense, counting and numerical discrimination are not synonymous because numerical discrimination does not require an ability to count.

EXERCISES

13-1: It is well established that accuracy of choosing the correct comparison stimulus in a DMTS task decreases as the duration of the delay (retention interval) increases. In the space below, draw and explain a graph depicting this functional relation.

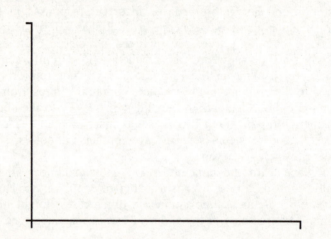

13-2: The *serial position effect* refers to the tendency for animals to recall items from the beginning and end of a list more accurately than those from the middle of the list. Draw and explain a graph that depicts the relation between recall and serial position. Be sure to come up with an appropriate definition for "recall."

13-3: In general, species differ in how long they can retain information across different delays in DMTS tasks. For example, humans can retain information longer than monkeys, which can retain information longer than pigeons. In the space below, draw, label, and explain a graph depicting the functional relations between retaining information and the duration of the delay. Draw the functions of all three species on the same graph. However, do not use "retaining information" as a label for one of the axes. Instead, come up with a plausible operational definition (i.e., something that can be quantified and measured) for "retaining information," and use this as the label for one of the axes.

13-4: Consider the following statement: *Accuracy on a DMTS task depends on the duration that the sample stimuli are presented.*

13-4.1: What do you think is a likely functional relation between accuracy of choosing the correct comparison stimulus and the duration of the sample stimuli? Explain your answer.

13-4.2: Draw a graph that depicts the relation between accuracy of choosing the correct comparison stimulus and the duration of the sample stimuli.

13-5: Rats seem remarkably resistant to having the short-term or working memory of their behavior on the radial-arm maze disrupted. This resistance was shown by allowing rats to visit 4 arms of an 8-arm maze, each of which was baited with food. After eating the food from 4 of the arms, the rats were removed from the maze and returned to their home cages. After 4 hours in their cages (the retention interval), the rats were returned to the maze, and promptly visit first the 4 arms that still contained food. In other words, they did not make the mistake of revisiting the arms that they had previously depleted. Various control conditions showed that this accuracy was not due to olfactory or visual cues related to the food, nor to other scent or visual marking of the maze.

13-5.1: What do you think might happen to the rats' memory if they were required to perform an explicit task while off the maze rather than simply "sitting" in their home cages?

13-5.2: How might the similarity between the radial-arm maze task and a task they were required to perform while off the maze affect the accuracy of their behavior when they were returned to the maze?

13-5.3: In the space below, draw a graph that depicts a plausible functional relation between the type of task the rats performed during their time off the maze and the accuracy of their memory for where food was still located on or previously depleted from the maze. Where needed, be sure to come up with appropriate operational definitions. [Hint: When thinking about types of tasks, try to think of a task that is in some way quantitatively similar to the radial arm-maze task, e.g., have the rats spend time on mazes with different numbers of arms.]

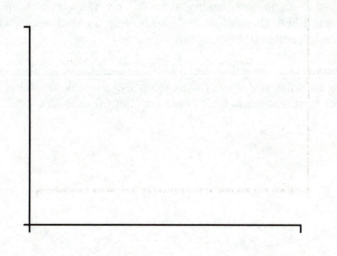

13-5.4: If these results were obtained, what would they tell us about the rats' memory?

13-6: The graph below depicts data from what is often referred to as the *peak procedure* for studying temporal discrimination. In this case, rats were presented on some trials with a tone, which signaled that either an FI 20-sec schedule was in effect or that no reinforcement would occur. On other trials, the rats were presented with a light, which signaled that either an FI 40-sec schedule was in effect or that no reinforcement would occur. On those instances in which reinforcement did not occur, the trial terminated after 80 sec.

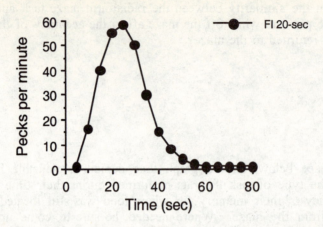

13-6.1: The data for what happened during the tone on those trials in which reinforcement did not occur are presented on the graph above. Given what you know about the scalar property of temporal discrimination, extend the results shown in the graph by drawing a curve (on the same graph) depicting how response rate likely changed across time during those trials in which the light was on and reinforcement did not occur.

13-6.2: In the curve you drew for the FI 40-sec schedule, explain why the peak is, depending on what you drew, (a) as steep as the peak for the FI 20-sec schedule, (b) steeper than this peak, or (c) broader (flatter) than this peak.

13-7: The *bisection procedure* is another common way of studying temporal discriminations. In this procedure, the animal is presented with a signal of various durations. After the signal is over, two levers (in the case of rats) are inserted into the experimental chamber. Pressing one of the levers is rewarded if the signal was the shortest in the range of durations used for the signals. Let's call this the Short lever. Pressing the other lever is rewarded if the signal was the longest in the range of durations being used. Let's call this the Long lever. Pressing either lever is not rewarded if the duration of the signal is other than these extremes. The behavior of interest is the probability of pressing the Long lever as a function of the duration of the signal. (Conversely, the dependent measure could be the probability of pressing the Short lever; it doesn't matter which one is used.)

The table below shows the probability of pressing the Long lever as a function of different durations of the signal. Another way of looking at this is that when the rat presses the Long lever, it is indicating that the duration of the signal falls into the "long" category. When the signal is short (e.g., 2 sec), the rat almost never presses the Long lever. That is, the rat does not indicate that the 2-sec signal belongs in the "long" category. However, when the signal is 8 sec, the rat almost always presses the Long lever, indicating that this duration belongs in the "long" category.

Time (sec)	Probability of Pressing "Long"
2	0.10
3	0.20
4	0.50
5	0.75
6	0.85
8	0.90

13-7.1: Complete the table below. [Hint: Note that you are providing probabilities of pressing the Short rather than the Long lever.]

Time (sec)	Probability of Pressing "Short"
2	
3	
4	
5	
6	
8	

13-7.2: In the space below, plot the data from the table in exercise **13-7**. As usual, clearly label all axes and specify the units of measurement (if there are any).

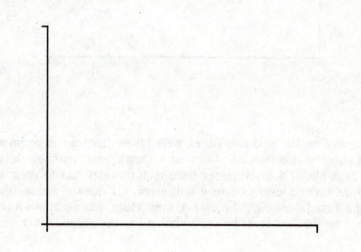

13-7.3: What is the indifference point (i.e., the duration at which the signal is equally often assigned into the "long" and "short" categories)?

13-7.4: Assuming that the rats which produced the data in the tables above were used in a new experiment, complete the table below. [Hint: Consider the scalar property of temporal discriminations.]

Time (sec)	Probability of Pressing "Long"
20	
30	
40	
50	
60	
80	

13-7.5.: In the space below, plot the data from the tables in exercises **13-7** and **13-7.4** in such a way that the scalar property is illustrated.

13-8: The data in the table on the next two pages were taken from an experiment in which rats had to press a lever at least *x* number of times and then press another lever once to receive reinforcement. For example, if 8 leverpresses were required, rats had to press one lever at least 8 times before pressing the second lever to earn a reinforcer. If the rat pressed the second lever after too few presses on the first lever (e.g., 6 presses), then there was no reinforcer and the rat had to make another 8 presses on the first lever before switching to the second lever.

Required Length of Run	Length of Run	Probability of a Run of x Presses
	1	0.02
	2	0.03
	3	0.13
	4	0.24
	5	0.26
	6	0.18
4	7	0.08
	8	0.04
	9	0.01
	10	0.005
	11	0.0027
	12	0.0014
	13	0.0009
	3	0.0008
	4	0.008
	5	0.01
	6	0.02
	7	0.04
	8	0.11
	9	0.15
8	10	0.19
	11	0.17
	12	0.14
	13	0.07
	14	0.05
	15	0.02
	16	0.01
	17	0.007
	18	0.004

(table continued on next page)

Required Length of Run	Length of Run	Probability of a Run of *x* Presses
	7	0.007
	8	0.01
	9	0.02
	10	0.05
	11	0.07
	12	0.13
12	13	0.16
	14	0.15
	15	0.14
	16	0.1
	17	0.06
	18	0.04
	19	0.03
	20	0.02
	21	0.01

13-8.1: Plot the data from the above table in the space below. Label your graph carefully!

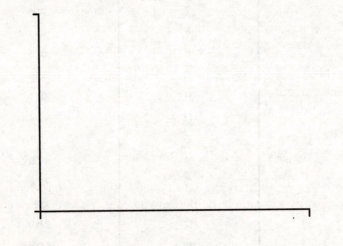

13-8.2: If you have plotted the data correctly, then you should be able to notice something interesting about the peak (i.e., the number of presses after which the rat is most likely to switch to the second lever). What is interesting about the location of the peak?

13-8.3: What, if anything, does this tell us about rats' counting abilities? What, if anything, does this tell us about the contingencies of reinforcement?

13-9: Imagine a hungry pigeon trying to decide whether to peck at a key when a particular stimulus is shown on the key. To be concrete, let's suppose that one of the four stimuli shown below is projected on the key for 30 sec. After the 30 sec elapses, another one of the four stimuli is projected for 30 sec, and so on for 30 minutes each day. What happens when the bird pecks at the key depends on the stimulus. When two of them are projected, pecks are reinforced with food according to a VI 15-sec schedule; when the other two are projected, pecks are never reinforced.

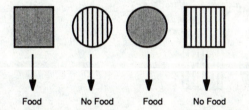

Not surprisingly, we expect the pigeon to learn the discrimination and eventually peck at the positive stimuli (i.e., those associated with food) and not peck, or peck much less, at the negative stimuli (i.e., those not associated with food).

13-9.1: Describe in words what you think the bird learned. (There is more than one way to answer this question.)

13-9.2: Someone tells you, or perhaps you thought of it on your own, that the pigeon's behavior accords to a simple rule. Can you conceive and state such a rule?

13-9.3: How would you convince a friend that your rule actually describes how the pigeon is *behaving* in this experiment?

13-9.4: Suppose that another bird is exposed to the same stimulus set but different contingencies of reinforcement -- see the figure below. State a rule that describes what this bird might have learned at the end of training.

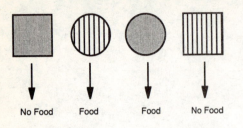

13-9.5: As in the previous exercise, state a rule that describes what a bird exposed to the contingencies summarized in the figure below might have learned at the end of training.

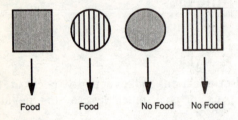

13-9.6: Assume that we label the dimensions as in the figure below. We can identify each stimulus by its coordinates. Thus, the filled circle would be designated as S1+C1 because it has shape S1 and color C1. Explain why the rule you stated in exercise **13-9.2** may be written as: "If C1 peck the key; otherwise do not peck."

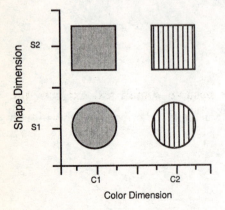

13-9.7: Write the corresponding rules for exercises **13-9.4** and **13-9.5**.

13-10: You can now deal with a slightly more complex stimulus set. Instead of 4 stimuli, the pigeon experiences 9 stimuli. These are shown in the figure below. The stimuli enclosed in the reverse L-shaped box are the ones associated with reinforcement; the others are associated with extinction. Assume that the bird learns the discrimination.

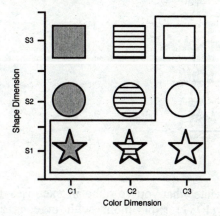

13-10.1: With reference to the figure above, how might we find a rule which includes, as it were, the positive stimuli and excludes the negative ones?

13-10.2: How might we find a rule which includes the positive stimuli and excludes the negative ones for the following figure?

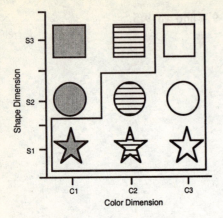

13-10.3: How might we find a rule which includes the positive stimuli and excludes the negative ones for the next figure?

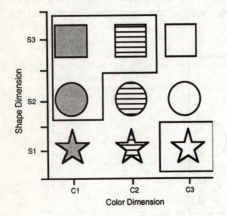

13-10.4: How would you relate what you've done in exercises **13-10** to **13-10.3** to Vaughn and Herrnstein's (1987) experiment with pigeons and the concept of "tree?" [Hints: How many dimensions would you need the classify the stimulus set? What would the equivalent of our enclosed stimuli look like? What rule might capture the positive instances and exclude the negative ones?]

13-10.5: Concept learning is a matter of controversy; the topic is difficult and its investigation relatively recent. Briefly discuss some limitations of our approach in exercises **13-9** and **13-10**.

14

CHOICE AND PREFERENCE: THE BASICS OF THE MATCHING LAW

Major topics covered in the exercises of this chapter:

Matching law, concurrent variable-ratio variable-ratio schedules, concurrent variable-interval variable-interval schedules

What is the matching law?

Consider some of the simplest choice situations: In a casino, a gambler chooses to pull either the Left or the Right arm of a slot machine, a 'two-armed bandit'; on a farm with two barns, a rat in search for food chooses to visit either the Left or the Right barn; in a laboratory, a hungry pigeon chooses to peck either the Left or the Right key in a Skinner box. After each choice, the subject may obtain a reinforcer -- the gambler may win a jackpot, the rat may find a piece of bread, and the pigeon may earn a bit of grain. Finally, the gambler, the rat and the pigeon can make hundreds of choices in relatively short amounts of time and play their respective choice games for many consecutive days.

The *matching law* is a statement relating the choices made to each alternative to the reinforcers obtained from these alternatives *after the subject has experienced the choice situation for a long time* (i.e., after the organism has made many choices). To put it differently, the matching law is a statement relating choices made and reinforcers obtained at the steady state (i.e., when there are no further changes in behavior). For the preceding examples, choices and reinforcers are summarized in Table 14.1.

Table 14.1

Behavior (B)	→	Reinforcers (R)
Pull Left arm, B_1 Pull Right arm, B_2	→ →	Jackpots for pulling Left arm, R_1 Jackpots for pulling Right arm, R_2
Search the barn on the Left, B_1 Search the barn on the Right, B_2	→ →	Bread in the Left barn, R_1 Bread in the Right barn, R_2
Peck Left key, B_1 Peck Right key, B_2	→ →	Grain from pecking Left key, R_1 Grain from pecking Right key, R_2

As you can see, there are four numbers to consider for each example:
[1]   The number of times alternative 1 was chosen. We will call this number, B_1.
[2]   The number of times alternative 2 was chosen. We will call this number, B_2.
[3]   The number of reinforcers obtained from alternative 1. We will call this number, R_1.
[4]   The number of reinforcers obtained from alternative 2. We will call this number, R_2.

The matching law states that:

$$B_1/(B_1+B_2) = R_1/(R_1+R_2)$$

In everyday language, the matching law says that the proportion of behavior allocated to an alternative equals or 'matches' the proportion of reinforcers obtained on that alternative. At a gross and intuitive level, this captures our experiences of spending more time doing those things that pay off better (i.e., more often). Returning to the equation, note that each side of the equation is a *proportion*. Thus, $B_1/(B_1+B_2)$ is the proportion, or fraction, of the total responses produced on alternative 1, and $R_1/(R_1+R_2)$ is the proportion, or fraction, of the total reinforcers obtained from alternative 1.

Because an understanding of the matching law requires that information and implications are mastered incrementally, we turn our attention next to the exercises and provide additional information interspersed among the exercises. Because of the cumulative nature of this material, it is imperative that you understand an exercise before moving onto the next exercise. This is one of those instances where there is not much point in moving onto a later exercise without understanding the preceding exercises.

EXERCISES

14-1: Check your understanding of the 'ingredients' of the matching law by filling in the blanks or circling the correct option within the {braces} in the questions below. Assume that B_1 and B_2 are not both zero and make the same assumption regarding R_1 and R_2.

14-1.1: Because both $B_1/(B_1+B_2)$ and $R_1/(R_1+R_2)$ are proportions, their values can never be greater than _____ or less than _____ .

14-1.2: If $B_1/(B_1+B_2) = 0$, then this means the subject {never/always} chose alternative {1/2}. Stated another way, it means that the subject {never/always} chose alternative {1/2}.

14-1.3: If $B_1/(B_1+B_2) = 1$, then this means the subject {never/always} chose alternative {1/2}. Stated another way, it means that the subject {never/always} chose alternative {1/2}.

14-1.4: If $B_1/(B_1+B_2) = .5$, then this means that the subject allocated

_____ .

14-1.5: If $R_1/(R_1+R_2) = 0$, then all reinforcers came from alternative _____ .

14-1.6: If $R_1/(R_1+R_2) = 1$, then the value of R_2 must be _____ and all reinforcers came from alternative _____ .

14-1.7: If $R_1/(R_1+R_2) = .5$, then this means that the subject earned

_____ .

14-1.8: With reference to the proportions in the matching equation, explain why the law is called the *matching* law.

14-2: Fill in the missing value in the table below to obtain matching:

Responses on Left (B_1)	150	Reinforcers from Left (R_1)	15
Response on Right (B_2)	440	Reinforcers from Right (R_2)	

14-3: Given that $B_1 = 3000$ and $R_1 = 450$, provide two solutions that will yield matching by filling in the blanks in the table below. It is important to note that, although there are infinite solutions that will result in matching, any solution must retain the key property of the matching law -- that the proportion of choices of alternative 1 must equal the proportion of reinforcers obtained from that alternative. The important message is this: **The matching law is a statement concerning two *proportions*, not the absolute numbers per se.**

	Responses on Left (B_1)	3000	Reinforcers from Left (R_1)	450
Solution 1:	Response on Right (B_2)		Reinforcers from Right (R_2)	
Solution 2:	Response on Right (B_2)		Reinforcers from Right (R_2)	

14-4: Could the matching law be expressed as $B_2/(B_1+B_2) = R_2/(R_1+R_2)$? Explain.

14-5: Suppose the results displayed in the table below were obtained in an experiment.

Rewards (per hour)		Responses (per hour)		$R_1/(R_1+R_2)$	$B_1/(B_1+B_2)$
Key 1	Key 2	Key 1	Key 2		
6	34	214	3504		
7	35	266	3063		
14	27	1784	3917		
21	21	2008	1998		
35	6	4182	451		
40	0	4797	0		

14-5.1: Complete the table above by filling in the open cells. [Hint: If you don't know how to start, begin by (a) identifying B_1, B_2, R_1, and R_2 and then (b) computing the two ratios or proportions.]

14-5.2: Plot the response and reinforcer proportions on a graph in which $R_1/(R_1+R_2)$ is the horizontal axis and $B_1/(B_1+B_2)$ is the vertical axis. When labeling the values on your axes, remember that you are plotting proportions and that these have specific upper and lower limits (see exercise **14-1.1**).

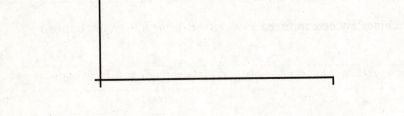

14-5.3: In the same graph, plot a line showing matching, i.e., $B_1/(B_1+B_2) = R_1/(R_1+R_2)$.

14-5.4: Interpret the graph by focusing on whether the deviations between the observed values (i.e., the actual data you plotted in exercise **14-5.2**) and the values predicted by the matching law (i.e., the line you drew in **14-5.3**) are large, whether deviations are systematic (i.e., consistently above or below the matching), and whether the matching law provides a good description of the obtained values.

14-6: Although it might not seem like it, all we have covered up to this point are the very basics of matching and the study of choice. We move now to exercises that will help us understand when and why matching does and does not occur. We begin with a brief discussion of the matching law and concurrent VR-VR schedules of reinforcement.

Consider the following game. If you pull the left arm of a two-armed slot machine, you receive a jackpot with probability 0.1; however, if you pull the right arm, then you receive a jackpot with probability 0.05. Another way to characterize this choice game is by noting that to win a jackpot by pulling the left arm, you will need to pull it, *on average*, 10 times. Where did the number 10 come from? Well, a probability of 0.1 means than the event in question (in this case, the jackpot) has a 1 in 10 chance of occurring with each pull of the arm (i.e., 1 in 10 chances is another way of saying $1 \div 10$, 1/10, or 0.1). After winning a jackpot, the very next pull of the left arm might yield another jackpot, but it might also require 20 pulls of that arm before the next jackpot occurs. In other words, we do not know *exactly* how many pulls of the left arm are needed before the next jackpot occurs. It could be 1, 20, 5, 38, or many other numbers. What we do know is that *on average* it takes 10 pulls of the left arm before it will yield a jackpot. Similarly, a probability of 0.05 for the right arm means that, *on average*, 1 jackpot will occur after 20 pulls of the right arm (and 1 in 20 is the same as $1 \div 20$, 1/20, or 0.05).

To summarize, there are two interchangeable ways of describing this choice game. We can provide [1] the probabilities of reinforcement per response (in the examples above, the probability of reinforcement for pulling the left arm is 0.01; the probability of reinforcement for pulling the right arm is 0.05) or [2] the average number of responses per reinforcement (in the example above, 10 pulls of the left arm for a reinforcer and 20 pulls of the right arm for a reinforcer). One is the *reciprocal* of the other.

Of these two interchangeable ways, psychologists who study choice prefer to talk about the average number of responses per reinforcer because it is seems more concrete than talking about probabilities. Moreover, we recognize in the 'average number of responses per reinforcer' an old acquaintance, the *variable ratio (VR)* schedule. In fact, a VR-10 schedule is a schedule in which each response has a probability of 0.1 of being reinforced.

14-6.1: Check your understanding of the preceding ideas by filling in the empty cells of the table:

Reinforcement probability per response		*Average* number of responses per reinforcer	
Arm 1	Arm 2	Arm 1	Arm 2
0.01	0.05	VR-100	VR-20
1		VR-1	VR-67
0.3		VR-3.3	VR
	0	VR	VR
p	q	VR-1/p	VR
		VR-x	VR-y

A concurrent variable ratio x variable ratio y schedule, abbreviated Conc. VR-x VR-y, is a choice schedule in which alternative 1 has associated with it a VR-x schedule and alternative 2 a VR-y schedule. The letters x and y are positive numbers that indicate how many responses on average are required for reinforcement.

14-7: Fill in the blanks and circle the correct option within the {braces}: In a Conc. VR-5 VR-45 schedule, _____ responses to alternative 1 are needed {always/on average} for 1 reinforcer from that alternative, and _____ responses to alternative 2 are needed {always/on average} for 1 reinforcer from that alternative.

14-8: Now consider a Conc. VR-10 VR-20 schedule. Let's explore what the matching law predicts in this choice situation. We need to begin by determining R_1 and R_2 because once we get these numbers we can compute $R_1/(R_1+R_2)$. And, given that we know that $B_1/(B_1+B_2) = R_1/(R_1+R_2)$, we can then predict the proportion of responses to each alternative.

   14-8.1: A feedback function relates the rate of reinforcement to the rate of responding. Before drawing a feedback function (exercise **14-8.2**), complete the table below by filling in the blank cells. Completing the table will help you see how response rate is related to reinforcement rate during a VR 10 schedule.

VR 10	
Average number of responses per minute, B_1	**Average number of reinforcers received, R_1**
0	0
5	
10	1
20	
40	
80	8
160	

   14-8.2: Plot the feedback function for the VR-10 schedule with response rate on the horizontal axis and reinforcement rate on the vertical axis. Also, write a figure caption that describes your graph.

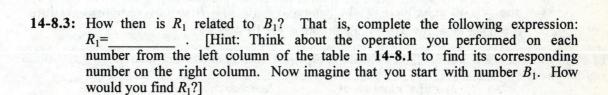

14-8.3: How then is R_1 related to B_1? That is, complete the following expression: $R_1=$_____ . [Hint: Think about the operation you performed on each number from the left column of the table in **14-8.1** to find its corresponding number on the right column. Now imagine that you start with number B_1. How would you find R_1?]

14-8.4: Alternative 2 is a VR-20 schedule. How then is R_2 related to B_2? That is, $R_2=$_____ . Therefore,

$$B_1/(B_1+B_2) = R_1/(R_1+R_2)$$
$$= (B_1/10)/(B_1/10 + B_2/20)$$
$$= 2B_1/(2B_1 + B_2)$$

That is,

$$B_1/(B_1+B_2) = 2B_1/(2B_1 + B_2)$$

which, after cross-multiplying, simplifies to

$$B_1B_2 = 2B_1B_2$$

But a number cannot equal twice itself unless that number is 0. Therefore, the number B_1B_2 must equal 0, which means that either $B_1=0$ (which indicates exclusive preference for alternative 2, the VR-20 schedule) or $B_2=0$ (which indicates exclusive preference for alternative 1, the VR-10 schedule).

The result that concurrent VR-VR schedules yield exclusive preference for one alternative is always true except when the VRs are equal. But in this case you can prove that any choice proportion is consistent with the matching law.

14-8.5: Given a Conc. VR-10 VR-10 schedule, repeat the derivation in exercise **14-8.4** to show that $B_1/(B_1+B_2) = B_1/(B_1+B_2)$.

Here is the important conclusion. In a Conc. VR-x VR-y schedule, the matching law predicts *exclusive preference* for one alternative, even though it cannot predict which alternative the subject will prefer. Although most subjects will develop exclusive preference for the richer alternative (i.e., the one that yields more reinforcement per response or the VR-10 schedule in the Conc. VR-10 VR-20 example above), either preference is consistent with the matching law.

14-9: In a Conc. VR-5 VR-25 choice situation, a person or animal chooses alternative 1, 1000 times and alternative 2, 200 times.

14-9.1: Are these choice results consistent with the matching law? Explain.

14-9.2: How many rewards for each alternative is the subject likely to have received?

14-9.3: Is the following statement accurate: "Because 1000/(1000+200) equals 25/(25+5), the matching law was exactly verified."? Explain.

14-10: Let's now turn our attention to Conc. VI VI schedules, a classic schedule for studying matching and choice behavior. We begin by considering a situation in which you have two e-mail accounts with distinct addresses (Address 1 and Address 2). Each account allows only one message in the mailbox at any given time. (In other words, you cannot accumulate messages. Each time you check your mail, there is never more than one message waiting for you.) When you decide to check if you have mail, you choose one of the accounts and click its icon. Getting a message is a reinforcer for the response of clicking on the icon. Suppose also that because more of your friends write to Address 1, more messages go to that address than to Address 2. Specifically, let's say you receive, *on average*, one message at Address 1 every 3 minutes, and, *on average*, one message at Address 2 every 6 minutes.

If you can remember what you learned about schedules of reinforcement, then you will realize that in the situation just described the reinforcement schedule for each alternative is a variable-interval or VI schedule. More accurately, because there are two schedules of reinforcement in operation at the same time, the situation may be described as a concurrent VI 3-min VI 6-min schedule and abbreviated Conc. VI 3-min VI 6-min.

14-10.1: Guess what the matching law predicts for this choice situation (i.e., a Conc. VI 3-min VI 6-min like the one controlling your e-mail address checking behavior). [Hint: The question is asking: What is $B_1/(B_1 + B_2)$? But where should you start? Begin by trying to guess, based on intuition, how R_1 is related to B_1. Do you think that a person trying to maximize rewards should check only one account? If you said 'yes,' then why? If you said 'no,' then how should you distribute your behavior? Remember, if you determine R_1 and then R_2, you will know the answer to the question because $B_1/(B_1 + B_2) = R_1/(R_1 + R_2)$, and you are trying to determine $B_1/(B_1 + B_2)$. Conc. VI-VI schedules are trickier than Conc. VR-VR schedules because there is a temporal component in VI schedules. However, careful and patient thinking might allow you to guess the answer. Don't worry about being right at this time. The next exercise will help you derive the answer.]

14-10.2: Now let's examine the relation between behavior and reinforcement on VI schedules more carefully. Begin by recalling that, on a VI 3-min schedule, a reinforcer becomes available after an average of 3 min has elapsed since the previous reinforcer. If you repeatedly click on Address 1's icon very rapidly, say at a rate of 600 (or even more) clicks per hour, then the most e-mails you can get per hour is _____ .

14-10.3: What is the most number of e-mails you can get per hour if you click on Address 1's icon at a rate of 120 clicks per hour? _____

14-10.4: What is the most number of e-mails you can get per hour if you click on this icon very slowly, say, 1 click per hour? _____

14-10.5: Assuming that the schedule of reinforcement does not change, under which conditions of responding (clicking) will you get less than 20 e-mails per hour?

14-10.6: From your answers to exercises **14-10.1** through **14-10.5**, you should be able to complete the table below and then plot the feedback function for a VI 3-min schedule. Begin by completing the table.

VI 3-min	
Average number of responses per hour, B_1	Average number of reinforcers per hour, R_1
0	0
1	
10	10
20	20
120	
600	
1000	20

14-10.7: Plot the feedback function for a VI 3-min schedule with response rate along the horizontal axis and reinforcement rate on the vertical axis.

14-10.8: Although the VI feedback function is not as simple as a straight line, you should note that for a large range of response rates, reinforcement rate is approximately equal to _____ reinforcers per hour. In other words, to an approximation, the reinforcement rate R_1 is independent of the response rate B_1 and thus $R_1 =$ _____ .

14-10.9: The above reasoning is also valid for Address 2 (the VI 6-min schedule). Only by clicking Address 2's icon less than _____ times per hour will you get fewer than 10 reinforcers per hour. Thus, for all practical purposes we can consider R_2 constant and $R_2 =$ _____ .

We're almost done! From the matching equation, $B_1/(B_1+B_2) = R_1/(R_1+R_2)$, we get

$$B_1/(B_1+B_2) = R_1/(R_1+R_2)$$
$$= 20/(20 + 10)$$

That is,

$$B_1/(B_1+B_2) = 2/3$$

The matching law predicts that the fraction of your clicks on Address 1's icon will be 2/3. That is, for every 300 clicks that you make, about 200 will be on Address 1's icon and 100 will be on Address 2's icon. (If this does not seem reasonable, then you need to redo the questions in exercise **14-10** and/or speak with your instructor.) Here is an important conclusion: **The matching law predicts a nonexclusive (partial) preference on Conc. VI VI schedules.**

14-11: A rat presses two levers to obtain food pellets according to a Conc. VI 60-sec VI 60-sec schedule. At the steady state the rat responds at a constant rate of 360 leverpresses per hour overall (i.e., summed across both levers).

14-11.1: According to the matching law, what proportion of its responses will be on lever 1 and what proportion will be on lever 2?

14-11.2: Approximately how many rewards will the rat get in one hour from the two levers combined?

14-11.3: Why is the rat *not* better off responding exclusively on one of the levers?

14-12: A pigeon pecks two response keys. Its pecks to key 1 are reinforced on a VI 45-sec schedule; its pecks to key 2 are reinforced on a VI 15-sec schedule. Both schedules are in operation at the same time; this is a Conc. VI 45-sec VI 15-sec schedule. After prolonged exposure to this situation (i.e., at the steady state), what proportion of the pigeon's responses will be on key 1 and which proportion will be on key 2? [Hint: Convert each VI schedule into number of reinforcers per hour.]

14-13: Why do Conc. VR VR schedules generally yield exclusive preferences whereas Conc. VI VI generally yield partial preferences? [Hint: Think about what happens to the probability of reinforcement on one alternative while the subject responds on the other alternative.]

15

EXTENSIONS OF THE MATCHING LAW

Major topics covered in the exercises of this chapter:

Deviations from matching, bias, undermatching, overmatching, the ideal-free distribution, alternative expression of matching, applications of the matching law

Deviations from matching

Strict matching, $B_1/(B_1+B_2) = R_1/(R_1+R_2)$, which is what we have discussed so far, is not always observed. There are three types of systematic, as opposed to random, deviations that are commonly found in the study of choice: (a) *bias*, (b) *undermatching*, and (c) *overmatching*. **To detect these deviations you must plot the data in the following form: $B_1/(B_1+B_2)$ on the vertical axis and $R_1/(R_1+R_2)$ on the horizontal axis.**

   Bias occurs when a person or animal has a preference for one alternative and this preference is unrelated to the ratio of reinforcement. To detect bias, look at choice proportion when the reinforcement proportions are equal, that is, $R_1/(R_1+R_2) = 0.5$. Three cases are possible:

[1]   If $B_1/(B_1+B_2) > 0.5$, then there is bias *for* alternative 1;
[2]   If $B_1/(B_1+B_2) = 0.5$, then there is *no* bias;
[3]   If $B_1/(B_1+B_2) < 0.5$, then there is bias *against* alternative 1 (i.e., a bias for alternative 2).

   Undermatching occurs when the choice proportion is *less* extreme than the reinforcement proportion. Another way to say this is that the ratio $B_1/(B_1+B_2)$ is always closer to 0.5 than the ratio $R_1/(R_1+R_2)$.

   Overmatching occurs when the choice proportion is *more* extreme than the reinforcement proportion. That is, the ratio $B_1/(B_1+B_2)$ is always farther from 0.5 than the ratio $R_1/(R_1+R_2)$.

EXERCISES

15-1: Examine the following graphs, and use them to answer the remaining questions in this exercise.

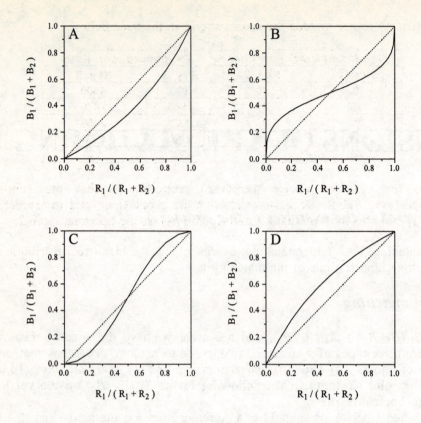

15-1.1:   Using the definitions provided above, identify which graphs depict bias for alternative 1, bias against alternative 1, undermatching, and overmatching. Circle the correct option in the {braces}.

[1]   Bias for alternative 1: Graph {A, B, C, and/or D}

[2]   Bias against alternative 1 (i.e., bias for alternative 2):
Graph {A, B, C, and/or D}

[3]   Undermatching: Graph {A, B, C, and/or D}

[4]   Overmatching: Graph {A, B, C, and/or D}

15-1.2:   Using the graph for undermatching, trace over the appropriate line or curve that illustrates that the ratio $B_1/(B_1+B_2)$ is always closer to 0.5 than the ratio $R_1/(R_1+R_2)$. If you would find it helpful, add additional labels to the graph and provide a brief description of what you are illustrating.

15-1.3:   Using the graph for overmatching, trace over the appropriate line or curve that illustrates that the ratio $B_1/(B_1+B_2)$ is always farther from 0.5 than the ratio $R_1/(R_1+R_2)$. If you would find it helpful, add additional labels to the graph and provide a brief description of what you are illustrating.

15-2: An experiment on choice yielded the results shown in the table below.

Reinforcements per hour		Responses per hour	
Key 1	Key 2	Key 1	Key 2
0	40	100	4600
10	30	1540	2900
20	20	2500	2450
30	10	2750	1500
40	0	4500	150

15-2.1: Plot the observed choice (response) proportion against the reinforcement proportion. [Hint: Begin by calculating the proportions and remember to place $B_1/(B_1+B_2)$ on the vertical axis and $R_1/(R_1+R_2)$ on the horizontal axis.]

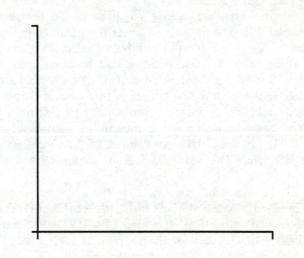

15-2.2: Compare the results of your plot with those predicted by the matching law. Was there systematic deviation from matching? Explain and, if yes, identify what the deviation is.

15-3: The matching law may be expressed in two equivalent ways. One is the equation already presented, which we call the *proportion* version because it expresses an equality between two proportions.

$$B_1/(B_1 + B_2) \quad = \quad R_1/(R_1 + R_2)$$

To derive the second version, we assume that none of the four variables (B_1, B_2, R_1, and R_2) equals 0. Here is the derivation, step by step:

Start with:	$B_1/(B_1 + B_2)$	$=$	$R_1/(R_1 + R_2)$
cross-multiply:	$B_1(R_1 + R_2)$	$=$	$(B_1 + B_2) R_1$
remove parentheses:	$B_1R_1 + B_1R_2$	$=$	$B_1R_1 + B_2R_1$
cancel common terms:	B_1R_2	$=$	B_2R_1
divide by B_1B_2:	R_2/B_2	$=$	R_1/B_1

The last equation represents the second way to express the matching law. To understand what it says, we need to understand first what the ratio R_1/B_1 means. To that end, let us think about the gambling example from Chapter 14. The number of times the gambler pulled the slot machine's left arm is represented by B_1; let us say $B_1 = 100$. The number of jackpots received from pulling that arm is represented by R_1; let us say $R_1 = 5$. Given these two numbers, how would you estimate the probability that the left arm will yield a jackpot when pulled? You don't need a course in statistics to realize that your best estimate is the ratio R_1/B_1, which in this case is 5/100. Thus, on average, 100 pulls of the left arm yields 5 jackpots, or that the probability of getting a jackpot after pulling the left arm is 0.05 or 5%. You could be wrong -- the probability setting of the left arm on the slot machine could be 0.06 or 0.04, not 0.05, but the value 0.05 is your best estimate of the jackpot occurring after pulling the left arm. The value 0.05 is the *obtained* probability, not the *scheduled* probability.

The second version of the matching law says that the obtained probability of reinforcement for choice 1 (represented by R_1/B_1) equals the obtained probability of reinforcement for choice 2 (represented by R_2/B_2). More generally, then, the matching law states that the subject making the choices will allocate its behavior to the various alternatives in such a way that (at the steady state) the probabilities of reinforcement across the alternatives will be the same. We call this second version of the matching law the *reinforcement probability* version.[1]

At this time, you may be wondering why you need to know the two versions of the matching law. Good question! The two versions are different views of the same thing. However, just as you learn more about a sculpture when you look at it from different directions, you also learn more about the matching law when you express and see it in different ways. Furthermore, it is also the case that some problems --as you will soon find out! -- are best handled with the *proportion* version, whereas others are best handled with the *reinforcement probability* version. Let's get to it.

15-3.1: Imagine that a pigeon chooses to peck the left key 500 times and that the bird received 50 rewards for this response. What is the obtained probability of a reinforced response, R_1/B_1? _____

15-3.2: Although you do not know the values of B_2 and R_2, can you say something about their values? If yes, what is it?

---

[1] There is a third way to express the matching law, i.e., $B_1/B_2 = R_1/R_2$. This might be called the *odds* version because the ratio B_1/B_2 can be interpreted as the odds of behavior 1 to behavior 2 and similarly for the ratio R_1/R_2. We will not explore this version any further.

15-4: Starting with the probability version of the matching law, derive the proportion version.

15-5: In this exercise, we examine an application of the matching law to the behavior of a tennis player choosing between whether to hit a lob or a passing shot. We also revisit a few ideas and concepts from previous chapters on operant conditioning.

> **15-5.1:** Imagine that you are playing tennis with a friend. From previous experience you have learned that the more you use passing shots, the less effective the next one will be. Similarly, the more you use lobs, the less effective the next lob will be. Taking into account the behavior of your opponent, provide a brief rationale for these contingencies of reinforcement. Be sure to use concepts that you have learned in the psychology of learning class such as reinforcement, punishment, stimulus discrimination.

> **15-5.2:** For our purposes here, assume that your choices of shots are restricted to passing shots and lobs. That is, your shots consist of only one or the other. Based on your previous games with the same opponent, your coach calculated the contingencies of reinforcement for the two alternatives. These are summarized in the table below. For example, the numbers in the second row were determined by observing that during one match you used 40 passing shots and 160 lobs, for a total of 200 shots (choices). The proportion of passing shots is therefore 40/200 = 0.2. Of the 40 passing shots, 10 were successful; therefore, the probability of success for a passing shot was 10/40 = 0.25. Of the 160 lobs, only 16 were successful; therefore, the probability of success for a lob was 16/160 = 0.1. The remaining rows were obtained in similar ways.

Fill the top row of the table with the variables that you used in stating the matching law. [Hint: The probability of success for passing shots or lobs is neither $R_1/(R_1 + R_2)$ nor $R_2/(R_1 + R_2)$.]

Passing shots		Lobs	
Proportion	**Probability of success**	**Proportion**	**Probability of success**
0.1	0.275	0.9	0.05
0.2	0.25	0.8	0.1
0.4	0.20	0.6	0.2
0.5	0.175	0.5	0.25
0.6	0.15	0.4	0.3
0.8	0.10	0.2	0.4
0.9	0.075	0.1	0.45

15-5.3: Plot all data in one graph with the "proportion of passing shots" on the horizontal axis and the 'probability of success' on the vertical axis. Where do you put the 'proportion of lobs'? [Hint: What is the relationship between the proportion of passing shots and the proportion of lobs? Is there some way that they could share a common axis and scale?]

15-5.4: At what proportion of passing shots is the matching equilibrium of the game? (Equilibrium, in this case, means that your proportion of passing shots to lobs is such that you could not be more successful by changing the proportion of these shots.) Explain.

15-5.5: Plot and label the equilibrium point, A, on the graph you plotted in exercise **15-5.3**. Then, describe why no other point is consistent with matching.

15-6: The matching law is the most robust finding obtained to date in the study of choice. But to improve our understanding and broader significance of this law we will examine one of its biological relatives. This exercise is also an excellent way to improve your ability to draw and interpret graphs, to understand functional relations, and to think about the concept of equilibrium. Again, read carefully, be patient and persistent, and ask your instructor or teaching assistant for help if you need it. This is a long tutorial and problem.

Let's begin by imagining that you and a friend are throwing bits of bread or kernels of popcorn to pigeons in a public square. You throw an average of 30 pieces of food per minute. Twenty feet away, your friend throws an average of only 10 pieces of food per minute. There are 16 pigeons on the ground. Some of these birds will come to your area (let's call this Patch 1) and the remaining will go to the area where your friend is standing (let's call this Patch 2). Being a curious person, you set out to solve the following problem: How many pigeons will go to each patch such that, after a few minutes, each bird will be getting as much food as possible? To simplify the problem, we assume the birds live in a democratic society -- when more than one bird is in a patch they distribute evenly (i.e., share equally) the food in that patch. In other words, there is no competition between birds.

Before continuing, you may want to think about the problem for a few minutes and guess a solution based on a reasonable justification. The exercise will deepen your knowledge of graphs and the matching law.

15-6.1: Imagine that only one bird goes to Patch 1 (which means that the other 15 go to Patch 2). In this situation the lonely but lucky bird in Patch 1 will get all the food that you are throwing (i.e., 30 pieces per minute).

Patch 1	
Number of birds (let's call it *x*) **(from 0 to 16)**	**Rate of food intake (let's call it *y*)** **(bits of bread per bird per minute)**
$x = 1$	$y = 30/1$ or 30

In the table above, x is the number of birds that go to Patch 1, and y is the number of bits of food each bird gets in 1 minute. Now, what happens if, instead of only 1 bird, 2 birds go to your patch and divide the food evenly between them? In this case, $x = 2$ and $y = 30/2$ or 15. In the table below, fill in the blank cells while paying particular attention to the row that shows the general case (labeled x).

Patch 1	
Number of birds (*x*)	**Rate of food intake (*y*)**
0	Undefined
1	30/1
2	
3	
...	...
x	$y =$
...	...
14	
15	
16	

15-6.2: Let's now turn to your friend and see what is happening in Patch 2. If $x = 1$, that is, when only one bird goes to *your* patch, then 15 go to Patch 2. Because they evenly divide the 10 pieces of food, each one will get $z = 10/15$ bits of food per minute. Following the same reasoning for the case $x = 2$, $x = 3$, and so on, complete the table on the next page.

Patch 1		Patch 2	
Number of birds	Rate of food intake	Number of birds	Rate of food intake
0	undefined	16	
1	30/1	15	
2		14	
3		13	
...	...	...	...
x	y =	16 - x	z =
...	...	...	...
14		2	
15		1	
16		0	undefined

Now look back at the table above and see what you wrote for the general case. Copy it in the table below.

	Food in Patch 1 (y)	Food in Patch 2 (z)
Birds in Patch 1 (x)	y =	z =

15-6.3: In the space below, plot the two functions (one for Patch 1 and one for Patch 2) showing how the amount of food a bird eats is related to the number of birds in a patch. [Hint: Define the horizontal axis as *birds in patch 1* and the vertical axis as *rate of food intake*. Pay attention to the upper and lower limits of these axes.]

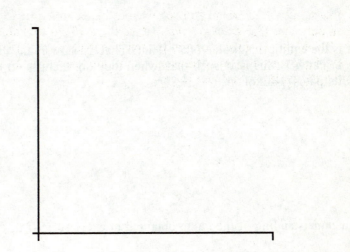

15-7: At this point, it is worth reminding ourselves of the problem we are trying to solve: We want to know how many pigeons will go to each patch such that, after a few minutes, each pigeon will be getting as much food as it can get. When each bird is getting as much food as it can get, then it will not be tempted to leave its patch because there is nothing to gain. The situation in which every bird is, loosely speaking, as happy as it could be and does not want to move, is an *equilibrium* condition. We can therefore restate the problem you are trying to solve as follows: What is the equilibrium value of x? (No need to answer just yet; you'll be asked to do so in exercise **15-7.5**.)

15-7.1: To find the equilibrium value of x, look at your graph from exercise **15-6.3** and imagine that only one bird is in your patch. Then, do the following: Locate the rate of food that the bird in Patch 1 is getting, and then label this point A1.

15-7.2: Locate the rate of food that each one of the 15 birds in Patch 2 is getting, and then label this point B1.

15-7.3: Should any pigeon move from its patch? (In other words, can any bird improve its situation?) If so, how many should move? Explain your answer by referring to the graph in exercise **15-6.3**.

15-7.4: Now consider the opposite case: 15 pigeons are in Patch 1 and only 1 pigeon is in Patch 2. Should any bird move? Explain your answer by referring to the graph in exercise **15-6.3**.

15-7.5: What is the equilibrium value of x? [Hint: That is, how many birds will eventually settle in Patch 1 (this is x) such that, when they do, there is no reason for a bird to leave its patch?] Explain.

15-8: To check your understanding of the value obtained in exercise **15-7.5**, do the following:

15-8.1: Create an equation to find the exact value of x at equilibrium. [Hint: Look back at the table you completed in exercise **15-3.2**. Study how the rate of food intake changes as a function of the number of birds in the two patches. Now look at the general case. Use those values of "rate of food intake" to come up with an equation to find the exact value of x at equilibrium.]

15-8.2: At equilibrium, how much food is each bird getting in Patches 1 and 2?

15-8.3: See if you can generalize what you have learned: Imagine that Patches 1 and 2 deliver food at rates r_1 and r_2, respectively, and that there are N birds in the park. What is the equilibrium value for x?

You should recognize in the last equality the now familiar *matching law*. What you have just derived is what biologist call the *ideal free distribution*. It bears a close relation to what psychologists call the *matching law*.

REFERENCES

Aesop's fables (1999). New York: Grosset & Dunlap.

Bloom, B. S. (1956). *Taxonomy of educational objectives: Cognitive and affective domains*. New York: David McKay.

Keller, F. S., and Schoenfeld, W. N. (1995). *Principles of psychology*. Acton, MA: Copley Publishing Group. (Original work published 1950.)

James, W. (1890). *The principles of psychology*. New York: Holt.

Pavlov, I. P. (1927). *Conditioned reflexes*. (G. V. Anrep, trans.). London: Oxford University Press.

Vaughn, W., Jr., and Herrnstein, R. J. (1987). Choosing among natural stimuli. *Journal of the Experimental Analysis of Behavior, 47*, 5-16.

INDEX

THE PSYCHOLOGY OF LEARNING:
A STUDENT WORKBOOK